A Commitment to Teaching

A Commitment to Teaching

Toward More Efficacious Teacher Preparation

Edited by Patrick M. Jenlink

ROWMAN & LITTLEFIELD
Lanham • Boulder • New York • London

Published by Rowman & Littlefield
An imprint of The Rowman & Littlefield Publishing Group, Inc.
4501 Forbes Boulevard, Suite 200, Lanham, Maryland 20706
www.rowman.com

6 Tinworth Street, London SE11 5AL, United Kingdom

Copyright © 2020 by The Rowman & Littlefield Publishing Group, Inc.

All rights reserved. No part of this book may be reproduced in any form or by any electronic or mechanical means, including information storage and retrieval systems, without written permission from the publisher, except by a reviewer who may quote passages in a review.

British Library Cataloguing in Publication Information Available

Library of Congress Cataloging-in-Publication Data

Library of Congress Control Number: 2020931521

ISBN: 978-1-4758-5482-4 (cloth)
ISBN: 978-1-4758-5483-1 (pbk.)
ISBN: 978-1-4758-5484-8 (electronic)

A Commitment to Teaching: Toward More Efficacious Teacher Preparation is dedicated to present and future generations of teachers that enter the classroom with commitment to teaching.

Contents

Preface		ix
Acknowledgments		xiii
1	Ensuring Teachers' Commitment and Sense of Self-efficacy: The Role of Teacher Preparation *Patrick M. Jenlink*	1
2	The Relationship of Hours of Teacher Preparation Programs' Field Experiences and Pre-Service Teacher Candidates' Sense of Teaching Efficacy *Alison Reddy, Shana Pribesh, Leigh Butler, and Charlene Fleener*	13
3	How Reflectivity Impacts Teacher Candidates' Self-efficacy *Sherri M. Weber and Julie J. Henry*	33
4	A Framework for Measuring Algebra Teacher Self-efficacy *Trena L. Wilkerson, M. Alejandra Sorto, William A. Jasper, Sandra Cooper, Winifred Mallam, Colleen M. Eddy, Yolanda A. Parker, Sarah Quebec Fuentes, Judy M. Taylor, and Elizabeth K. Ward*	45
5	Development of Chinese Teachers' Self-efficacy in a Professional Learning Community *Qing Gao and Jian Wang*	73
6	The Role of Self-efficacy and Other Characteristics of Elementary Mathematics Teachers: A Model to Predict Student Achievement *James A. Telese, Zhidong Zhang, and Maria E. Diaz*	93

7	Teachers' Knowledge, Perception, Sense of Self-efficacy and Role in Mental Health for Middle School Students *Federico R. Guerra, Jr., Ashwini Tiwari, Nancy Peña Razo, and Lionel Javier Cavazos Vela*	113
8	Epilogue: Toward More Efficacious Teacher Preparation *Patrick M. Jenlink*	135
About the Contributors		143

Preface

The commitment that drives teachers to enter and remain in the teaching profession has been of great interest among researchers and teacher educators. Commitment, as a form of motivation, is multifaceted, influenced by both intrinsic and extrinsic motivators. Self-efficacy plays a key role in teacher commitment to entering and remaining in the profession. The level of confidence that individuals have manifests in teacher self-efficacy to effectively determine instructional strategies for diverse learners in the classroom. Student success reinforces teacher confidence and commitment, intersecting with self-efficacy beliefs.

Importantly, drawing on theoretical notions of teacher learning and teacher cognition (thinking and beliefs) in order to critically examine the perspective of teachers themselves and their preparation and practice experiences are essential to addressing reimagining preparation programs. There is, in the experiences of pre-service and novice teachers, a rich and important knowledge of how the "self" evolves in relationship to self-efficacy and the emerging of teacher efficacy as a necessary element of teaching and learning.

Teacher self-efficacy, and the presence of teacher efficacy, in teacher preparation and practice, is fundamental to preparing teachers for the public school classroom. As a construct, teacher self-efficacy beliefs are an integral aspect of the teaching process. While many authors refer to teachers' sense of self-efficacy for teaching, meaning their beliefs about their ability to perform the actions necessary to teach, many others have identified a specific form of self-efficacy pertaining to teaching. These have been called teaching or teacher efficacy.

Understanding the relationship of teacher self-efficacy and teacher efficacy is directly related to teaching and learning, and equally important, to student learning and success. Teachers in classrooms across the larger educational landscape are met with challenges of students' cognitive and emotional differences, challenges that place the teacher in a crucial role of ensuring that all students are successful, including students from linguistically and culturally diverse backgrounds and students with special needs.

Teacher self-efficacy is an important motivational construct that shapes teacher effectiveness in the classroom. Self-efficacy beliefs serve as a key motivational force in the cognitive system. Self-efficacy is considered to lead individuals from knowledge to action. Teachers with a high level of teacher self-efficacy have been shown to be more resilient in their teaching and likely to try harder to help all students to reach their potential. In contrast, teachers with a low level of teacher self-efficacy have been found to be less likely to try harder to reach the learning needs of all their students. It is for this reason that the investigation of the development of teacher self-efficacy in pre-service teacher education is important. During this time pre-service teachers undergo a clinical or practicum experience that serves as "apprenticeship of learning" that is situates the pre-service teacher in the experiential reality of the classroom.

Teacher self-efficacy relates to the beliefs teachers hold about their own perceived capability in undertaking certain teaching tasks and meeting the challenges in the classroom. Teacher self-efficacy is a belief in one's capabilities to organize and execute the course of action required to produce given attainments. Self-efficacy therefore influences thought patterns and emotions that enable classroom actions. In the context of education, teacher self-efficacy is considered a powerful influence on teachers' overall effectiveness with students.

Understanding teacher self-efficacy and teacher efficacy in the context of teacher preparation and practice requires a research-based perspective on the nature of "efficacy" and the cognitive and emotional "self" of the teacher in relation to the needs of students. Teacher behavior, as foundational to teaching and learning, is influenced by the individual's beliefs regarding two classes of expectations: an outcome expectation as a person's estimate that a given behavior will lead to certain outcomes and an efficacy expectation as a conviction that one can successfully execute the behavior required to produce the outcome. Teacher efficacy is "normative" to successful teaching and learning and lends to teacher understanding and confidence as well as teacher and student learning and success. How teacher preparation programs perceive and ground the experiences of preparation and clinical practice lends to the success of preparing highly efficacious teachers for the classroom.

A Commitment to Teaching: Toward More Efficacious Teacher Preparation introduces the reader to a collection of thoughtful works by authors that represent current thinking about self-efficacy and teacher preparation. Each chapter focuses on self-efficacy and the preparation of teachers who will enter classrooms to instruct the next generation of students. Chapter 1 opens the book with a focus on self-efficacy and its relationship to teaching and learning in the classroom, providing the reader with an introduction. The authors of chapters 2–9 present field-based research that examines self-efficacy in teacher preparation and practice. Each chapter offers the reader an examination of teacher self-efficacy in educator preparation and practice based on formal research that provides the reader with insight into how the research study was conducted as well as the findings and conclusions drawn with respect to self-efficacy and teacher preparation and practice. Finally, chapter 8 presents an epilogue that focuses on the future of efficacious teacher preparation.

Acknowledgments

The initial idea for this book began as a conversation among colleagues focused on a concern for the importance of self-efficacy as foundational to preparing teaching. Specifically, we focused on concerns evident in current teacher preparation programs that knowledge of how the "self" evolves in relationship to self-efficacy and the emerging of teacher efficacy. The concern we fostered was the need to ensure that the next generation of teachers demonstrate efficacious behavior in the classroom and in their teaching.

In our conversations, we examined teacher efficacy as "normative" to successful teaching and learning and how it lends to teacher understanding and confidence as well as teacher and student learning and success. We recognized that using a subject-specific framework for investigating teachers' self-efficacy could give researchers, teacher educators, and teacher practitioners a window into the ways in which an emphasis on self-efficacy influences the work that they do with students.

Acknowledgment and thanks goes to the contributing authors whose research offers insight and thoughtful considerations for understanding the need to examine the meaning of self-efficacy as related to teacher preparation and practice, and the need for a deep understanding of the complexities of fostering self-efficacy and preparing the efficacious teacher.

The authors bring the welcomed perspective of theorists and researchers as well as their own field-based research to the discourses presented in the book. Without the contributing authors, this book would not have been possible. The authors of the chapters examining self-efficacy and educator preparation bring their considerable experience to bear on interpreting the complexity, challenges, and problems associated with preparing each new generation of teachers that bring a commitment to teaching and learning.

Gratitude is extended to the external reviewers who took time out their busy schedules to review and provide comments and suggestions on the chapters. Acknowledging the value of the chapters and offering constructive feedback was invaluable, as was the affirmation by reviewers for both the need and the importance of a book committed to self-efficacy and the preparation of efficacious teachers with commitment to teaching each new generations of teachers.

Likewise, gratitude is extended to Tom Koerner and the editorial staff at Rowman & Littlefield Education for their vision in seeing the value of a book on teacher self-efficacy that draws into specific relief the need to advance an understanding of how focusing on self-efficacy as a phenomenon central to teacher self-efficacy presents new challenges for teacher preparation and practice in public schools and college classrooms.

As well, thanks to the production staff at Rowman & Littlefield are in order for their ever-vigilant efforts to move the book through to completion. Working with a quality publisher and the folks that do the work to translate a manuscript into a completed book is a rewarding experience.

Finally, gratitude goes to Stephen F. Austin State University for supporting this project and enabling the realization of a work that will shape educator preparation for years to come.

Chapter One

Ensuring Teachers' Commitment and Sense of Self-efficacy

The Role of Teacher Preparation

Patrick M. Jenlink

Teacher commitment and self-efficacy are "normative" to successful teaching and learning and lends to teacher understanding and confidence as well as teacher and student learning and success. Commitment and self-efficacy are strongly related (Chesnut, 2017; Kozlowski & Salas, 2010). How teacher preparation programs perceive and ground the experiences of preparation and clinical practice with respect to commitment and self-efficacy lends to the success of preparing highly efficacious teachers for the classroom.

Teacher commitment to the teaching profession is complex and multifaceted in nature, embodying social, cognitive, and cultural dimensions.[1] Teacher commitment is concerned with a teacher's amount of psychological attachment to the teaching profession (Coladarci, 1992). The decision to enter and remain in the teaching profession emerges from beliefs about the future self of the teacher, personal beliefs about what the teacher can successfully and competently perform, expectations that are held about the nature of entering a teaching position, the belief in its utility, and emotional awareness (Chesnut, 2017). Importantly, commitment to one's profession and one's self-efficacy as a teacher are intertwined.[2] Career-related decisions such as commitment to teaching are influenced by self-efficacy beliefs in one's ability to succeed.

Bandura (1997), in his social theory of cognition, defined self-efficacy as the "beliefs in one's capacity to organize and execute the courses of action required to produce given attainments" (p. 3). In essence, Bandura posited that an individual's beliefs about the ability to do something has significant consequence as to whether or not an individual will persist and actually accomplish the tasks assigned. As Bandura (1997) further asserted, teachers' commitment to work and learning of their students could be attributed to their belief in their ability to successfully enhance student learning.[3] In turn, teachers' sense of self-efficacy for teaching depends on their beliefs about their ability to perform the actions necessary to teach (Fives, 2003).

Teachers' self-efficacy is highly correlated with their well-being which, in turn, affects teaching commitment and the decision to enter the teaching profession (Chesnut & Cullen, 2014). In essence, a teacher's beliefs about the ability to do something has significant consequence as to whether or not a teacher entering the profession (and the classroom) will persist and actually accomplish the tasks of engaging students in learning, resulting in successful learner outcomes.[4]

SELF-EFFICACY AND COMMITMENT

Coladarci (1992), in examining teachers' sense of efficacy and commitment to teaching, found that teacher self-efficacy was one the strongest predictors of teacher commitment. Pendergast, Garvis, and Keogh (2011), in examining preservice teacher self-efficacy, noted that self-efficacy is related to student achievement and commitment to teaching. Beza (2016), in researching the path to more efficacious teacher preparation, found that "teacher efficacy, which is cognitive judgment that teachers hold regarding their capacity to take action and succeed, has a powerful influence on their teaching effectiveness" (p. 125). Commitment to teaching is a form of motivation; "teaching is multifaceted in that it is influenced by both intrinsic (e.g., self-efficacy, utility) and extrinsic motivators (e.g., workload, salary, politics)" (Chesnut, 2017, p. 171).[5]

Teacher self-efficacy and commitment to teaching are not generally innate. Self-efficacy and commitment to teaching are developed over time and in appropriate contexts, contexts such as teacher preparation, working with mentors in clinical settings, and the actual teaching experience. Teacher candidates enter teacher preparation programs with a recognized level of personal knowledge related to classrooms, schools, teachers, and instructional practices based on their own school experiences. Clark and Newberry (2019) noted that "teaching may be the only profession where candidates have the opportunity to see the job in action and bring these years of experience with them to their teacher education program" (p. 34).

As Tschannen-Moran and Woolfolk Hoy (2001) explained, supporting the development of teachers' self-efficacy is essential for preparing effective, committed, and enthusiastic teachers. The role that preservice teacher preparation programs play is important in the development of beginning teacher self-efficacy, identity as teacher, and commitment to the teaching profession. The role that teacher educators play is even more important, ensuring that preservice teachers are well prepared and provided with the critical experiences, knowledge, and understanding essential to shaping and retaining a high level of self-efficacy and commitment to teaching. The question is, what do teacher preparation programs need to do in order to ensure each candidate embraces self-efficacy and commitment as a teacher?

Efficacious Teacher Preparation

Preservice teacher education programs play a critically important role in the development of beginning teacher' self-efficacy and commitment. Teacher educators in preparation programs are charged with the responsibility of preparing preservice teacher candidates to become highly efficacious and committed teachers. This is equally important to teacher preparation globally (Beza, 2016; Canrinus, Helms-Lorenz, Beijaard, Buitink, & Hofman, 2012; Fathi & Rostami, 2018; Pendergast, Garvis, & Keogh, 2011; Svenja Vieluf, Kunter, & van de Vijver, 2013; Takahashi, 2011).

Along with the requisite content and pedagogical knowledge, teachers need to have a high level of confidence in their abilities to enact effective instructional practices that result in students' learning, motivation, and success in all aspects, for all students. Logically, teacher self-efficacy and commitment are associated with teacher persistence and retention (Zhang, Wang, Losinski, & Katslyannia, 2013). What is important to understand, as Tschannen-Moran and Woolfolk Hoy (2005) explain, is the differential antecedents of self-efficacy beliefs of preservice and novice teachers and more experienced teachers. The preservice teacher self-efficacy beliefs are generally in the early stages of formation. The point here is for teacher educators to understand the differential between their own self-efficacy beliefs and those of their students.

Teachers with high sense of self-efficacy work harder and persist longer when students are hard to teach (Woolfolk, 2008). They are also less likely to leave the profession prematurely (Fives, Hamman, & Oliverez, 2005). That is, teachers require a high level of self-efficacy for teaching, defined as a belief in one's own "capabilities to organize and execute courses of action required to successfully accomplish a specific teaching task in a particular context" (Tschannen-Moran, Woolfolk Hoy, & Hoy, 1998, p. 233). Toward the goal of developing a high sense of self-efficacy, understanding the nature of experiencing successes and failures, sources of efficacy, and external control factors are important to more efficacious preservice teacher preparation.

Experiencing Success and Failures

Chesnut (2017) explained "the malleability of confidence makes self-efficacy an optimal target for intervention in teacher education programs" (p. 171).

This malleability is essential to teacher preparation as well as when a teacher enters the classroom for the first time and experiences both successes and failures in the teaching and learning experience. Quintessential to success of the preservice teacher's preparation and sense of self-efficacy is for the teacher educator and the preservice teacher alike to understand how to initiate and maintain a course of behaviors leading to successful outcomes; such a course ensures strong self-efficacy beliefs during both successes and experiences of failure.

Equally important is understanding that failures will occur in classroom teaching and student learning, and that when met with failure, the teacher will experience a reduction in their expectations as self-efficacy beliefs are challenged concerning what they can do successfully as a teacher (Bandura, 1977a, 1986, 1993, 1997; Chesnut, 2017). Perceptions of classroom preparedness and confidence are best understood and articulated using the concept of teacher efficacy, which has been connected to positive teaching behaviors, to a willingness to remain in teaching, and to student achievement (Tschannen-Moran, Hoy, & Hoy, 1998).[6]

The preservice preparation experience of teachers that incorporates opportunities to observe and experience both successes and failures enables the future teacher to "receive information about [teacher] performances and make attributions about their successes and failures" (Chesnut, 2017, p. 171). Attributions regarding teacher performances most likely assist in calibrating self-efficacy beliefs and expectations about what the teacher can successfully accomplished in the classroom (Duffin, French, & Patrick, 2012; Schunk & Pajares, 2009; Settlage, Southerland, Smight, & Ceglie, 2009; Usher & Pajares, 2008).

Sources of Efficacy

Bandura (1986, 1991, 1995, 1997) identified four main sources that contribute to self-efficacy, which include mastery experiences, vicarious experiences, verbal persuasion, and emotional and physiological state. Usher and Pajares (2008), building on Bandura's work, noted that after completing academic tasks in preparation, preservice teachers "interpret and evaluate the results obtained, and judgments of competence are created or revised according to those interpretations" (p. 752).

The most powerful source contributing to preservice teacher self-efficacy is the mastery experience, previous mastery experiences, that is, previous experiences with succeeding or failing on activities that are similar to the current activity (Skaalvik & Skaalvik, 2016).[7] The school setting of the mastery experience, that is, rural, suburban, and urban, has an impact on the development of teacher self-efficacy. These experiences, for the preservice teacher, are the hands-on teaching opportunities of teaching in the classroom. Because mastery experiences are considered the most influential of all sources of efficacy, it is important that preservice teachers have ample mastery experiences to enhance self-efficacy beliefs (Fives et al., 2007; Hamman, Olivarez, Jr., Lesley, Button, Chan, Griffith, & Elliot, 2006; Knoblauch & Chase, 2015; Usher & Pajares, 2008).

Bandura (1997) categorized self-modeling as a vicarious experience. Self-modeling may occur in different contexts (e.g., observing other teachers mastering similar challenges) (Skaalvik & Skaalvik, 2016).[8] Clark and Newberry (2019), advancing Bandura's vicarious experience source of self-efficacy, explained vicarious as the act of imagining oneself teaching or watching someone model teaching, which is removed from the responsibility of teaching children. The benefit for preservice teachers with respect to vicarious experiences is the opportunities the preservice teacher has during their teacher education program to teach peers a lesson they have designed, or they have the opportunity to watch someone modeling a teaching skill; modeling has been found to be particularly influential (Beza, 2016; Johnson, 2010; Moulding, Stewart, & Dunmeyer, 2014; Pendergast, Garvis, & Keogh, 2011).

Moulding, Stewart, and Dunmeyer (2014), examining the influence of mentoring provided by the cooperating teacher during student teaching clinical experiences, determined that preservice teacher self-efficacy was significantly correlated to a form of verbal persuasion (e.g., social support from colleagues and the school administration) experienced in the mentoring and support relationship between the preservice teacher and mentor or administrator (Skaalvik & Skaalvik, 2016). Verbal persuasion influences the preservice teacher's perceived capability to enter the classroom and teach students with successful learning outcomes. Rots, Aelterman, Vlerick, and Vermeulen (2007) found that supervision and support provided by the teacher education faculty and mentors was related to higher preservice teacher self-efficacy. The impact of verbal persuasion is magnified when it closely follows a successful mastery experience (Wise & Trunnell, 2001).

The emotional and physiological state (e.g., a teacher noticing increased cardio response when facing emotional stress) in teaching is an awareness of the emotional and physical response while engaged in the teaching experience. Self-efficacy beliefs are informed by emotional and physiological states such as anxiety, stress, fatigue, and mood (Usher & Pajares, 2008). Importantly, for the preservice teacher in preparation, learning to interpret their emotional and physiological state during the teaching experience, as an indicator of personal competence, by evaluating their own performances under differing conditions contributes to enhancing self-efficacy beliefs. Strong emotional reactions to school-related tasks can provide cues to expected success or failure. High anxiety as well as other emotional states can undermine self-efficacy (O'Neill & Stephenson, 2012; Stephanou & Oikonomou, 2018).

Self-efficacy is a "situation specific construct and fluctuates depending on for instance the perceived difficulty of the task, which resources are available, the perception of obstacles, and the time allocated for the task" (Skaalvik & Skaalvik, 2016, p. 1787). Ensuring that the preservice teacher preparation focuses on mastery experiences, vicarious experiences, verbal persuasion, and an emotional and physiological state that is aligned with quality teaching and focused on strengthening self-efficacy beliefs is critical to the larger responsibility of preparing highly efficacious teachers (Clark & Newberry, 2019).

External Control

There are external control factors that impact teacher decisions to stay or leave the teaching profession.[9] These are important factors for preparing teachers and such factors may have an impact on teacher self-efficacy beliefs and levels of commitment to the profession of teaching. Skaalvik and Skaalvik (2010) in researching teacher burnout as a factor related to the integrity of self-efficacy beliefs noted that factors external to teaching puts limitations to what teachers can accomplish. There are factors external to teaching that put limitations to what teachers can accomplish. These factors may include standards and accountability requirements, standardized curriculum, and related state policy requirements.

External control is perceived to negatively impact teacher self-efficacy beliefs, including context (e.g., rural, suburban, urban; high poverty; etc.) and factors external to teaching (e.g., students' abilities and home environments) are equally if not more important to the students' learning than the influence that a teacher may have. Skaalvik and Skaalvik (2016) further explicate that different potential stressors predict emotional exhaustion, engagement, and motivation through different psychological processes. These stressors, coupled with external control factors, may influence teacher self-efficacy by their perception of stressors (obstacles) in the environment, which may make teaching more difficult to carry out in the school classroom.

Important to remember, as Tschannen-Moran & Woolfolk Hoy (2001) defined, self-efficacy is a teacher's "judgment of his or her capabilities to bring about desired outcomes of student engagement and learning, even among those students who may be difficult or unmotivated" (p. 783). When considering external control, self-efficacy determines how environmental opportunities and impediments are perceived and therefore influences teachers' goals, values, and behavior (Bandura, 2006). This point reiterates the importance of considering the sources of self-efficacy essential to teacher preparation and enacting those sources in the lessons and content as well as pedagogical knowledge embodied in the preparation experience.

CONCLUSIONS

When it comes to preservice teachers and their preservice teacher preparation programs, these programs are the primary if not the sole sources of their efficacy information. What the research demonstrates is that greater teacher self-efficacy leads to greater commitment and persistence, which leads to higher quality success in teaching students and in turn to student success, which in turn leads to greater self-efficacy not only for the teacher but equally important to greater self-efficacy for students.

Given that the initial and continued success of any preservice teacher as well as a more experienced teacher is in large measure defined by their perceived self-efficacy, and that those first experiences in teacher preparation programs and clinical settings seem to set the tone for professional growth in terms of knowledge and self-efficacy beliefs, it seems logical that teacher preparation programs should emphasize the development of higher self-efficacy beliefs and maintain these beliefs throughout their preparation program experiences, and into their first classroom teaching opportunity.

Considering the effects of teacher self-efficacy on their teaching behavior and the resultant student outcomes as learner, strengthening ways of preparing more efficacious teachers should be taken as an avenue by those preparing teachers as well as those teachers working to improve student learning outcomes in school classrooms. The preservice preparation program and the teacher educators therein have responsibility for ensuring both a more efficacious teacher preparation program and ensuring that preservice teachers have high levels of self-efficacy beliefs.

NOTES

1. Chesnut (2017) noted that, when considering commitment, drawn from the extant research, "studies on preservice teacher commitment to the profession tend to be based on a positive orientation to commitment (e.g., intention to enter the profession, intended years as a teacher); whereas, studies on inservice teacher commitment to the profession tend to be grounded in a negative orientation to commitment (e.g., emotional burnout, intentions to leave the profession, attrition). Given that quantitative investigations of commitment tend to rely on only one operational definition (e.g., psychological attachment, intentionality, burnout) per study, the

lack of guidance in the field about which is most appropriate undermines research efforts and limits the types of conclusions that can be drawn from otherwise thorough investigations" (p. 170).

2. The importance of self-efficacy intertwined with commitment is rooted in its ability to guide the decisions that teachers make in the course of their role as teachers. Decisions that ensure a high level of self-efficacy also serve to motivate a teacher. If one begins with Bandura's (1977) proposition that self-efficacy "determines whether coping behavior will be initiated, how much effort will be expended and how long it will persist in the face of aversive experiences" (p. 191), it is evident that self-efficacy aids teachers in the course of their professional life. The ability to persist in teaching requires a belief in one's self as teacher, which in turn has a positive impact on commitment.

3. Tschannen-Moran and Woolfolk Hoy (2001), in their extensive research on teacher efficacy and self-efficacy, elaborated on Bandura's (1997) definition, speaking to the nature of teacher judgment in teaching: "A teacher's efficacy belief is a judgment of his or her capabilities to bring about desired outcomes of student engagement and learning, even among those students who may be difficult or unmotivated" (p. 783).

4. Self-efficacy encompasses beliefs in one's ability to initiate and maintain the courses of action necessary for success; beliefs that are foundational to remaining committed to teaching. For the teacher committed to remaining in the class and teaching students, self-efficacy beliefs might manifest as a high level of confidence to provide alternative instructional strategies for children from linguistically and culturally diverse backgrounds and provide appropriate instructional adaptations for students with special needs (Chesnut, 2017). "Teacher self-efficacy extends to motivating students, teaching difficult concepts, learning content material, monitoring student behavior, and more" (Clark & Newberry, 2019, p. 33).

5. Working in unison with commitment, self-efficacy beliefs serve as a key motivational force in the cognitive system. Self-efficacy is considered to guide the teacher from knowledge to action. Bandura (1986) posited that self-efficacy is the central mediator of effort. That is, increased efficacy beliefs will lead to increased persistence and high levels of performance.

6. Experiencing failures could lead to negative self-perception regarding teaching abilities and consequently a lowered teaching confidence that can prevent teachers from making crucial connections with students.

7. Moulding et al. (2014) explained that "[e]nactive attainment is the actual personal successes or accomplishments of the individual, sometimes referred to as authentic mastery experience . . . which is the most powerful source of self-efficacy" (p. 60). Preservice field or clinical experiences, such as student teaching in actual school classrooms, are the most likely opportunity for preservice teachers to develop mastery by practicing the skills and actions of a teacher: the target task.

8. Self-modeled experiences may take many forms, particularly as regards modeling through forms of multi-media and playback of recorded vicarious experiences and are certainly intertwined with the judgments preservice teachers would make of their mastery experiences.

9. External control refers to factors external to teachers and their teaching practice, which puts limitations to what they can accomplish. Skaalvik and Skaalvik (2010) explain that external control "may also be conceptualized as a general measure of educational pessimism or optimism. Because external control may be confounded with teacher self-efficacy it is important to test how strongly [their] constructs are related and if they relate differently to school context variables and to teacher job satisfaction. One of the purposes of this study was to test relations between individual teacher self-efficacy" (p. 1060)

REFERENCES

Bandura, A. (1977a). Self-efficacy: Toward a unifying theory of behavioral change. *Psychological Review, 84*, 191–215.

———. (1986). *Social foundations of thought and action: A social cognitive theory.* Englewood Cliffs, NJ: Prentice-Hall.

———. (1991). Social cognitive theory. *Organizational Behavior and Human Decision Processes, 50,* 248–287.

———. (1993). Perceived self efficacy in cognitive development and functioning. *Educational Psychologist, 28*(2), 117–148.

———. (1995). Exercise of personal and collective efficacy in changing societies. In A. Bandura (Ed.), *Self-efficacy in changing societies* (pp. 1–45). New York, NY: Cambridge University Press.

———. (1997). *Self-efficacy: The exercise of control.* New York: W. H. Freeman.

———. (2006). Adolescent Development from an Agentic Perspective. In F. Pajares & T. Urdan (Eds.), *Self-efficacy beliefs of adolescents* (pp. 1–43). Greenwich, CN: Information Age Publishing.

Beza, A. (2016). The path to more efficacious teacher preparation: The role of adequate coursework and practicum factors. *International Journal of Science and Research Publications, 6*(8), 125–130.

Canrinus, E. T., Helms-Lorenz, M., Beijaard, D., Buitink, J., & Hofman, A. (2012). Self-efficacy, job satisfaction, motivation and commitment: Exploring the relationships between indicators of teachers' professional identity. *European Journal of Psychology of Education, 27,* 115–132.

Chesnut, S. R. (2017). On the measurement of preservice teacher commitment: Examining the relationship between four operational definitions and self-efficacy beliefs. *Teaching and Teacher Education, 68,* 170–180. http://dx.doi.org/10.1016/j.tate.2017.09.003

Chesnut, S. R., & Cullen, T. A. (2014). Effects of self-efficacy, emotional intelligence, and perceptions of the future work environment on preservice teacher commitment. *The Teacher Educator, 49*(2), 116–132. doi: 10.1080/08878730.2014.887168

Clark, S., & Newberry, M. (2019). Are we building preservice teacher self-efficacy? A large-scale study examining teacher education experiences. *Asia-Pacific Journal of Teacher Education, 47*(1), 32–47. doi: 10.1080/1359866X.2018.1497772

Coladarci, T. (1992). Teachers' sense of efficacy and commitment to teaching. *Journal of Experimental Education, 60*, 323–337.

Duffin, L. C., French, B. B., & Patrick, H. (2012). The Teachers' sense of efficacy scale: Confirming the factor structure with beginning pre-service teachers. *Teaching and Teacher Education, 28*, 827–834.

Fathi, J., & Rostami, E. S. (2018). Collective teacher efficacy, teacher self-efficacy, and job satisfaction among Iranian EFL teachers: The mediating role of teaching commitment. *Journal of Teaching Language Skills (JTLS), 37*(2), 33–64. DOI: 10.22099/jtls.2019.30729.2572

Fives, H. (2003, April). *What is teacher efficacy and how does it relate to teachers' knowledge?* Paper presented at the American Educational Research Association Annual Conference, Chicago, IL.

———. (2005, April). Does burnout begin with student-teaching? Analyzing efficacy, burnout, and support during the student-teaching semester. Paper presented at the Annual Meeting of the American Educational Research Association, Montreal, CA.

Fives, H., Hamman, D., & Olivarez, A. (2007). Does burnout begin with student-teaching? Analyzing efficacy, burnout, and support during the student-teaching semester. *Teaching and Teacher Education, 23*(6), 916–934.

Hamman, D., Olivarez, A., Jr., Lesley, M., Button, K., Chan, Y., Griffith, R., & Elliot, S. (2006). Pedagogical influence of interaction with cooperating teachers on the efficacy beliefs of student teachers. *The Teacher Educator, 42*, 15–29. http://dx.doi.org/10.1080/08878730609555391

Ho, I. T., & Hau, K. -T. (2004). Australian and Chinese teacher efficacy: Similarities and differences in personal instruction, discipline, guidance efficacy and beliefs in external determinants. *Teaching and Teacher Education, 20*, 313–323.

Johnson, D. (2010). Learning to teach: The influence of a university-school partnership project on pre-service elementary teachers' efficacy for literacy instruction. *Reading Horizons, 50*(1). Retrieved from http://scholarworks.wmich.edu/cgi/viewcontent.cgi?article=1003&context= reading_horizons

Knoblauch, D., & Chase, M. A. (2015). Rural, suburban, and urban schools: The impact of school setting on the efficacy beliefs and attributions of student teachers. *Teaching and Teacher Education, 45*, 104–114.

Moulding, L. R., Stewart, P. W., & Dunmeyer, M. L. (2014). Pre-service teachers' sense of efficacy: Relationship to academic ability, student teaching placement characteristics, and mentor support. *Teaching and Teacher Education, 41*, 60–66.

O'Neill, S., & Stephenson, J. (2012). Exploring Australians pre-service teachers sense of efficacy, its sources, and some possible influences. *Teaching and Teacher Education, 28*, 535–545. http://dx.doi.org/10.1016/j.tate.2012.01.008

Pendergast, D., Garvis, S., & Keogh, J. (2011). Pre-service student-teacher self-efficacy beliefs: An insight into the making of teachers. *Australian Journal of Teacher Education, 36*(12), 46–57. Retrieved from http://dx.doi.org/10.14221/ajte.2011v36n12.6

Redmon, R. J. (2007, October 5). *Impact of teacher preparation upon teacher self efficacy*. Paper presented at the Annual Meeting of the American Association for Teaching and Curriculum, Cleveland, Ohio.

Rots, I., Aelterman, A., Vlerick, P., & Vermeulen, K. (2007). Teacher education, graduates' teaching commitment and entrance into the teaching profession. *Teaching and Teacher Education, 23*(5), 543–556.

Schunk, D. H., & Pajares, F. (2009). Self-efficacy theory. In K. R. Wentzel & A. Wigfield (Eds.), *Handbook of motivation at school* (pp. 35–53). New York, NY: Routledge.

Settlage, J., Southerland, S. A., Smight, L., & Ceglie, R. (2009). Constructing a doubt-free teaching self: Teacher efficacy, teacher identity, and science instruction within diverse settings. *Journal of Research in Science Teaching, 46*(1), 102–125.

Siwatu, K. O., & Chesnut, S. R. (2014). The career development of preservice and inservice teachers: Why teachers' self-efficacy beliefs matter. In H. Fives & M. Gill (Eds.), *International handbook of research on teachers' beliefs* (pp. 212–229). New York, NY: Routledge.

Skaalvik, E. M., & Skaalvik, S. (2010). Teacher stress and teacher self-efficacy as predicators of engagement, emotional exhaustion, and motivation to leave the teaching profession. *Teaching and Teacher Education, 26*(4), 1059–1069. http://dx.doi.org/10.1016/j.tate.2009.11.001

———. (2016). Self-efficacy, efficacy and teacher burnout: A study of relations. *Creative Education, 7*(13), 1785–1799. doi: 10.4236/ce.2016.713182

Stephanou, G., & Oikonomou, A. (2018). Teacher emotions in primary and secondary education: Effects of self-efficacy and collective-efficacy, and problem-solving appraisal as a moderating mechanism. *Psychology, 9*, 820–875. doi: 10.4236/psych.2018.94053

Svenja Vieluf, S., Kunter, M., van de Vijver, F. J.-R. (2013). Teacher self-efficacy in cross-national perspective. *Teaching and Teacher Education, 35*, 92–103.

Takahashi, S. (2010). Co-constructing efficacy: A "communities of practice" perspective on teachers' efficacy beliefs. *Teaching and Teacher Education, 27*, 732–741.

———. (2011). Co-constructing efficacy: A "communities of practice" perspective on teachers' efficacy beliefs. *Teaching and Teacher Education, 27*, 732–741.

Tschannen-Moran, M., & Anita Woolfolk Hoy (2001). Teacher efficacy: Capturing an elusive construct. *Teaching and Teacher Education, 17*(7), 783–805.

———. (2005). The differential antecedents of self- efficacy beliefs of novice and experienced teachers. *Teaching and Teacher Education, 23*, 944–956.

Tschannen-Moran, M., Anita Woolfolk Hoy, & Wayne Kolter Hoy (1998). Teacher efficacy: Its meaning and measure. *Review of Educational Research, 68*(2), 202–248.

Usher, E. L., & Pajares, F. (2008). Sources of self-efficacy in school: Critical review of the literature and future directions. *Review of Educational Review, 78*, 751–796.

Wise, J., & Trunnell, E. (2001). The influence of sources of self-efficacy upon efficacy strength. *Journal of Sport and Exercise Psychology, 23*(4), 268–280.

Woolfolk, A. (2008). *Educational psychology: Active learning edition* (10th Ed.). Boston, MA: Pearson.

Zhang, D., Wang, Q., Losinski, M., & Katslyannia, A. (2013). An examination of preservice teachers' intentions to pursue careers in special education. *Journal of Teachers Education, 65*(2), 156–171.

Chapter Two

The Relationship of Hours of Teacher Preparation Programs' Field Experiences and Pre-Service Teacher Candidates' Sense of Teaching Efficacy

Alison Reddy, Shana Pribesh,
Leigh Butler, and Charlene Fleener

New teachers are tasked with continuously motivating students, meeting state and national standards, as well as preparing students to face the world on a global level (Erawan, 2011). Teachers must be able to make multiple and complex context specific decisions with increasingly diverse groups of students (Berry et al., 2010). Thus, teacher preparation programs are urged to focus on the best, most effective practices and experiences for preservice teacher candidates (Berry et al., 2010). Teacher self-efficacy—their feelings that they can teach—is proving to be a vital area in teacher performance (Erawan, 2011). But, the field of teacher preparation is still uncertain how to best foster teacher efficacy.

High quality teacher preparation programs' field experiences for prekindergarten to sixth-grade teacher candidates may serve as the link between preparing teachers for the real-world classroom and increasing teacher candidates' teaching efficacy. Field experiences create opportunities for teacher candidates to gain experience and practice ideas through observations and student teaching practices. Field experiences can be progressively integrated within methods classes and seen as encompassing concepts that are first introduced in methods courses. It is in field experiences that we expect future teachers to begin to move from understanding educational theory to combining the theory with actual practice (Clift & Brady, 2005).

SELF-EFFICACY AND TEACHING AND LEARNING

Swars (2005) explains that teacher efficacy involves effective classroom instructional strategies and the willingness to try new teaching ideas. Individual teacher efficacy is highly associated with teacher motivation (Bandura, 1977). Teachers who are willing to try new instructional ideas and persist when faced with obstacles are more likely to implement new approaches and to integrate the innovations into the classroom. These teacher behaviors are linked to academic success for students (Bruce & Ross, 2008).

Further, teachers with a strong sense of personal teaching efficacy tend to spend more time planning what they teach. They tend to be more open to new ideas and teaching approaches, set higher goals, are more willing to try new strategies, and persevere through the profession's challenges (Goddard, Hoy, & Hoy, 2000). Since teacher efficacy is context specific, teachers are not equally efficacious in all teaching situations. A teacher's efficacy depends on the subject they are teaching and the students they are instructing (Bandura, 1993, 1997; Goddard, Hoy, & Hoy, 2000). For example, a teacher may feel efficacious in teaching science but not efficacious in teaching language arts.

Educators' beliefs about their teaching capabilities can be strong indicators as to whether their students are successful academically. In fact, teachers who do not expect their students to succeed are less likely to put forth the effort to deliver the instruction needed to reach the students who are struggling academically (Tuchman & Issacs, 2011). Teachers of struggling students tend to give up quicker when faced with students' learning challenges. A teacher's teaching efficacy perceptions are predictive of student achievement (Bandura, 1993; Goddard, Hoy, & Hoy, 2000). This indicates self-efficacy beliefs in education can act as self-fulfilling prophecies, which can validate beliefs of students' capabilities and achievement (Tschannen-Moran & Woolfolk-Hoy, 2007). In other words, the teachers who believe they can positively influence students' learning have more success with their students' achievement than teachers with lower efficacy in teaching.

Field Experiences Relating to Teacher Efficacy

A plethora of teaching license preparation programs exist in thousands of schools of education. Programs often vary in their course requirements, hours and expectations of practica, and student teaching placements. According to Gurvitch and Metzler (2009), "authentic field experiences" are considered those that include a broad range of contextual factors in elementary through high schools. Experts view authentic field experiences as providing strong, real-world and in-class experiences to teachers in training. There also may be variant emphases on the relationships among the cooperating teacher, university supervisor, and teacher candidate.

According to Boyd, Grossman, Lankford, Loeb, and Wyckoff (2008), teachers with a variety of formal field experiences before beginning their teaching career have higher student achievement growth in their first year of teaching than those without these varieties of field-based experiences (Boyd et al., 2008). Most teacher education programs implement formal field experiences that provide preservice teachers opportunities to integrate knowledge and experience, practice teaching skills, and connect theory to practice (Liaw, 2009).

Formal field experiences include a variety of dimensions, including the length of experiences, the number and variety of placements, and the cooperating schools' contextual factors. These varying characteristics can drastically distinguish teacher education programs from one another. Boyd et al. (2008) explain that formal field experiences are vital to the teacher preparation experience. Preparation programs that provide opportunities for future educators to gain experiences in the classroom create better equipped and more effective first-year teachers. Candidates who actively participate in cooperating schools show evidence of an increase in teaching efficacy levels.

PROBLEM STATEMENT AND RESEARCH QUESTIONS

Although researchers agree that field experiences may be important and that teacher efficacy may be the key to early career teaching success, we know very little about the optimum amount of field experience and the purported relationship with efficacy. The purpose of this study is to examine various levels of programs' field experiences in different teacher preparation paths and the factors that contribute to preservice teacher candidates' teaching efficacy. This non-experimental, quantitative study involved 167 teacher candidates enrolled in one of five teacher license paths leading to their pre-kindergarten to sixth grade (PK–6) teaching license degree. All participants were enrolled in the same large public university in the mid-Atlantic region of the United States.

We addressed the problem of field experience in two ways. The first research question, "To what degree does the number of hours of elementary teacher candidates' field experiences influence their perceptions of their teacher efficacy?," looked at candidates' efficacy levels in a particular teacher preparation path as they accumulated more and more field experience hours. The second analysis compared candidates in five different teacher preparation paths that required vastly different amounts of field experience hour asking, "To what degree are there differences among teacher candidates' teaching efficacy beliefs who have completed their required license paths' field experiences?"

METHODS

This study used a non-experimental, quantitative design. All participants were enrolled in the same large public university in the mid-Atlantic region of the United States.

Participants

The study's population includes undergraduate and graduate teacher candidates in the United States. The study sample of 167 participants were working toward earning a PK–6 state's teaching license or had recently earned a teaching license a few months prior to the study from a large, four-year university in the eastern portion of the United States. The participants were enrolled in one of two teacher preparation programs and one of five license paths. Each path varies in the required number and duration of formal field placements.

Two Programs

The first preparation program is an approved state elementary education prekindergarten to sixth-grade teaching license program (Program 1). In this program, four license paths are offered. All four of the paths in Program 1 are approved by the state and result in a teaching license.

The second program is an alternative, state-funded Career Switchers license program to support professionals who want to become teachers on an accelerated timeline. Program 2 only has one path and results in a provisional state license. Table 2.1 displays the required hours and number of formal field experiences in each of the two teacher preparation programs and their corresponding license paths.

Five Paths

Path 1 is the 4+1 year path that results in a master of science in education for initial license elementary (PK–6). This five-year path (4+1 years) results in students earning a bachelor of science in interdisciplinary studies (IDS) and a master of science in education while earning a state teaching license. As an undergraduate in this path, 30 hours of classroom observation and between 70 and 110 hours of practica experience are required. As a master of science in education graduate student, an additional 150-hour practicum and 14 weeks of student teaching are completed. During the 30 hours of classroom observation, 15 of these hours are in a PK–3 classroom setting outside of the university and the other 15 hours are in a fourth- to sixth-grade classroom setting.

Table 2.1. The PK–6 Teaching License Paths and Required Field Experiences

	30 Hours of Classroom Observation (PK–3rd 50%) (4th–6th 50%)	40 Hours of Practicum (PK–3rd 50%) (4th–6th 50%)	70 Hours of Practicum (PK–3rd 50%) (4th–6th 50%)	150 Hours of Practicum (PK–3rd 50%) (4th–6th 50%)	14 Weeks of Student Teaching (PK–3rd 50%) (4th–6th 50%)
		Between Group Comparison for Question #2			
Program 1, Path 1 Interdisciplinary Studies degree plus Fifth Year MS in Education for Initial License Elementary (4+1 years)	x	x (depending on the year beginning program)	x	x	x
Program 1, Path 2 4+1 years Primary/ Elementary Emphasis—Post Baccalaureate license endorsement — IDS	x	x	x	x	x
Program 1, Path 2 — Non-IDS	x		x	x	x
Program 1, Path 3 MS in Education with Initial License	x		x	x	x
Program 1, Path 4 MS in Education with license degree designed for military families	x				x (10 wks)
Program 2, Path 5 Career Switchers Alternate Route Program earning a one-year provisional teaching license	x				

X = experience required with program's license path

The second field experience is a 40-hour practicum where the teacher candidate works with small groups of students in a classroom and continues to observe various teaching practices. Half of the 40 hours are with PK–3 students and the other half are with fourth- to sixth-grade students. The third field experience required in this path includes a 70-hour practicum. During the master's portion of this license path, the teacher candidates participate in a 150-hour practicum including 75 hours with pre-kindergarten to third-grade students and 75 hours with fourth- to sixth-grade students. Candidates in the first path also complete 14 weeks of student teaching. The student teaching field experience involves the teacher candidate giving small groups and whole class instruction in a variety of subject areas, managing classroom behavior, creating lesson plans, and implementing instructional strategies independently.

The study separated Path 1 into five tiers, A–G. These seven tiers include candidates at various placements during their field experiences. Tier A includes participants who completed a 70-hour practicum. These students transferred from a community college and may or may not have had the opportunity to do a 30-hour observation. Tier B included teacher candidates who completed a 30-hour observation and a 70-hour practicum, totaling 100 hours of field experiences. Tier C included participants who completed the 30-hour classroom observation, the 40-hour practicum, and the 70-hour practicum, which totaled 140 hours of formal field experiences. Tier D included participants who completed a 30-hour observation, 70-hour practicum, and 150-hour practicum, totaling 250 hours of formal field experiences. Tier E included teacher candidate participants who completed the 30-hour classroom observation, the 40-hour practicum, the 70-hour practicum, and the 150-hour practicum, totaling 290 hours of formal field experiences. Tier F included participants who completed the 30-hour classroom observation, the 70-hour practicum, and the 150-hour practicum, and 14 weeks of student teaching, totaling 810 hours of formal field experiences. Tier G included teacher candidate participants who completed the 30-hour classroom observation, the 40-hour practicum, the 70-hour practicum, and the 150-hour practicum, and 14 weeks of student teaching, totaling 850 hours of formal field experiences.

Candidates in Path 2 (License 1) result in earning a post baccalaureate license endorsement. These candidates are college students who wish to earn their teaching license *without* earning a master's degree. These candidates previously earned a BS or BA degree that did not result in a teaching license. Some of Path 2's candidates earned a BS or BA degree from a different university. After enrolling in the researched university's preparation program and path, candidates needed to complete a 30-hour observation field experience, a 150-hour practicum, and 14 weeks of student teaching.

Other candidates in Path 2 participated in the researched school's undergraduate program in interdisciplinary studies. These students completed equivalent education courses as Path 1 and participated in 30 hours of classroom observation, 260 hours (40+70+150 hours) of practica, and 14 weeks of student teaching. Path 2's practica hours are split by grade levels similarly to Path 1.

Path 3 (License 1) is designed for candidates who previously earned a non-education BS or BA degree from another university and wish to earn their master of science degree in education resulting in a teaching license. This master's program includes the same masters level education courses as Path 1 and similar formal field experiences. All of the required field experiences remain the same as Path 1 (30+70+150+14 weeks of student teaching).

Path 4 (License 1) is designed for candidates who are in the military, are military spouses, and/or select service personnel. This license path requires 30 hours of observation and 10–14 weeks of student teaching. The 40-, 70-, and 150-hour practica are not required for the degree. These participants earn a master of science in education degree after completing this path.

Path 5 (License 2) is an alternative route to the state's license called Career Switchers. Only one option for this license path is provided, which results in a one-year provisional state license. Only one 30-hour observation field experience is required in this path. A provisional license means that the candidate must complete other requirements before earning a five-year valid teaching license.

Measure: Teacher Sense of Efficacy Scale

We used valid and reliable questionnaire called the Tschannen-Morgan & Woolfolk-Hoy's (2001)'s Teachers' Sense of Efficacy Scale questionnaire. This questionnaire about teacher efficacy is designed to help educators gain a better understanding of the types of situations that create complications for teacher candidates and inservice teachers while teaching students. Teacher candidates had the option of choosing 1–9 for each response. A number 1 indicates the teacher candidate's belief that there is nothing that they can do to help a particular classroom circumstance, a number 3 indicates very little, a 5 indicates some influence, a 7 indicates having quite a bit of influence, and a 9 indicates the teacher can do a great deal about a particular classroom circumstance.

There are three subscales in the teacher efficacy questionnaire. These include efficacy of student engagement, efficacy of instructional strategies, and efficacy of classroom management. According to Tschannen-Morgan & Woolfolk Hoy (2001), Cronbach alpha scores for the teacher efficacy subscales were 0.94 for overall teachers' sense of efficacy, 0.87 for engagement, 0.91 for instruction, and 0.90 for management. Correlations between the subscales of engagement, instruction, and management were 0.58, 0.60, and 0.70, respectively ($p<0.001$).

Data Analysis

To analyze Research Question 1, "To what degree does the number of hours of elementary teacher candidates' field experiences influence their perceptions of their teacher efficacy?," candidates in Path 1: Interdisciplinary Studies program were separated according to the number of hours of field experiences they completed. Four separate regression analyses were run on the subscales of teaching efficacy as well as subscales and hours of field experiences.

Candidates' efficacy levels were compared within-group according to tiers A–G. Table 2.2 displays the 129 participants who responded from the Bachelor of Science in Interdisciplinary Studies +MS in Ed. license path (Path 1). Path 1's within-group participants were separated into tiers according to their progress in the program and their completed formal field experiences. Tier A ($n=5$) included participants who completed a 70-hour practicum. These students transferred from a community college and may or may not have had the opportunity to do a 30-hour observation. Tier B ($n=37$) included teacher candidates who completed a 30-hour observation and a 70-hour practicum, totaling 100 hours of field experiences. Tier C ($n=18$) included participants who completed the 30-hour classroom observation, the 40-hour practicum, and the 70-hour practicum, totaling 140 hours of formal field experiences. Tier D ($n=15$) included participants who completed a 30-hour observation, 70-hour practicum, and 150-hour practicum, totaling 250 hours of formal field experiences. Tier E ($n=13$) included teacher candidate participants who completed the 30-hour classroom observation, the 40-hour practicum, the 70-hour practicum, and the 150-hour practicum, totaling 290 hours of formal field experiences. Tier F ($n=26$) included participants who completed the 30-hour classroom observation, the 70-hour practicum, and the 150-hour practicum, and 14 weeks of student teaching, totaling 810 hours of formal field experiences. Tier G ($n=12$) included teacher candidate participants who completed the 30-hour classroom observation, the 40-hour practicum, the 70-hour practicum, and the 150-hour practicum, and 14 weeks of student teaching, totaling 850 hours of formal field experiences.

To analyze Research Question 2, "To what degree are there differences among teacher candidates' teaching efficacy beliefs who have completed their required license paths' field experiences?," a between-group One Way Analysis of Variance (ANOVA) was performed. Data were taken from the

Table 2.2. Within-Group Tiers A–G of Accomplishments from Path 1: Students Participating in the Bachelor of Science in Interdisciplinary Studies and Master of Science in Education 4 + 1 PK–Sixth-Grade Teacher License Path

Path 1 Tiers		Total Hours of Completed Field Experiences	30-hour Observation	40-hour Practicum	70-hour Practicum	150-hour Practicum	14-week Student Teaching
Tier A n=5	Within-group Regression Analysis - Path 1	70 hours			x		
Tier B n=37		100 hours	x		x		
Tier C n=18		140 hours	x	x	x		
Tier D n=18		250 hours	x		x	x	
Tier E n=13		290 hours	x	x	x	x	
Tier F n=26		810 hours	x		x	x	x
Tier G n=12		850 hours	x	x	x	x	x

Teacher Sense of Efficacy Scale's questionnaire responses to determine differences in degree programs' teacher efficacy.

For these analyses, questionnaire responses were analyzed from candidates who recently completed their final field experience from one of the five license paths (in most cases student teaching). A between group One Way Analysis of Variance (ANOVA) was also used to compare means of the three subcategories of the Teacher Sense of Efficacy Scale: efficacy of student engagement, efficacy of classroom management, and efficacy of instructional strategies.

Before running the analyses, we tested to see if the five basic assumptions of linear regression (and four of ANOVA) were met. The data were normally distributed, and the assumption of linearity is satisfied ($F = .720$, $p = .610$) (Glenn, Meyers, & Guarino, 2008). The Durbin-Watson statistic for overall efficacy was 2.74, thus satisfying the assumption of independence of errors. The homogeneity of variances were also not violated ($F(6,122) = 2.435, p = 0.029$).

Findings

To what degree does the number of hours of elementary teacher candidates' field experiences influence their perceptions of their teacher efficacy?

OVERALL TEACHING EFFICACY

The first research question was analyzed quantitatively through a within-group regression analysis among different stages of completed hours of field experiences. The linear regression indicates that the total number of hours of formal field experiences is a significant predictor of overall teaching efficacy. Table 2.3 shows a positive relationship between total hours of field experiences and overall efficacy, $F(1,127) = 8.392$, $p < 0.05$.

Table 2.3. Linear Regression for Overall Efficacy

	Sum of Squares	df	Mean Square	F	Sig.
Hours of Exp	6.306	1	6.306	8.392	.004[a]
Residual	95.422	127	.751		
Total	101.727	128			

a. Dependent Variable: Overall efficacy
b. Predictors: (Constant), Total Hours

Results for the coefficients for overall efficacy indicate the total hours of formal field experiences is a significant predictor of overall teaching efficacy with $\beta = .001$, $p = 0.004$. As the number of hours of completed field experiences increases so does overall teaching efficacy. The model summary of overall teaching efficacy indicates $R^2 = .062$. This indicates that approximately 6 percent of the total variance in overall teaching efficacy can be explained by the number of hours of formal field experiences. Six percent is considered to be a small effect.

Efficacy of Student Engagement

Efficacy of student engagement is a subscale of the overall efficacy questionnaire. The linear regression indicated the number of hours of formal field experiences is a significant predictor of the efficacy of student engagement. Results show a positive relationship between total hours of field experiences and efficacy of student engagement, with $F(1,127) = 5.228$, $p < 0.05$.

Efficacy of student engagement is positively related to the number of hours of fieldwork, $\beta = .001$, $p = 0.024$. As the number of hours of completed field experiences increase so does efficacy of student engagement. The model summary of efficacy of student engagement indicates $R^2 = .040$. This indicates that approximately 4 percent of the total variance in efficacy of student engagement can be explained by the number of hours of formal field experiences. Four percent is considered to be a slight effect.

Efficacy of Instructional Strategies

Efficacy of instructional strategies is a subscale of the overall efficacy questionnaire. The linear regression indicated the number of hours of formal field experiences is a significant predictor of the efficacy of instructional strategies, $F(1,127) = 5.090$, $p < 0.05$.

Findings indicate the coefficients of total hours of formal field experiences is a significant predictor of efficacy of instructional strategies with $\beta=.001$, $p = 0.026$. As the number of hours of completed field experiences increase so does efficacy of instructional strategies. The Model Summary of efficacy of instructional strategies indicates that $R^2 = .039$. This indicates that approximately 4 percent of the total variance in efficacy of instructional strategies can be explained by the number of hours of formal field experiences. Four percent total variance is considered to be a slight effect.

Efficacy of Classroom Management

Efficacy of classroom management is a subscale of the overall efficacy questionnaire. The linear regression indicated the number of hours of formal field experiences is a significant predictor of the efficacy of classroom management showing a positive relationship between total hours of field experiences and efficacy of classroom management, $F(1,127) = 12.940$, $p < 0.05$.

The coefficients of efficacy of classroom management indicates the total hours of formal field experiences is a significant predictor of efficacy of classroom management with $\beta = .001$, $p = 0.000$. As the number of hours of completed field experiences increase so does efficacy in classroom management. The model summary of efficacy of classroom management indicates that $R^2 = .092$. This indicates that 9 percent of the total variance in efficacy of classroom management can be explained by the number hours of formal field experiences. Nine percent is considered to be a small effect.

To what degree are there differences among teacher candidates' teaching efficacy beliefs who have completed their required license paths' field experiences?

OVERALL TEACHING EFFICACY

Participants in the IDS 4+1 year master of science in education license path (Path 1) had the highest mean efficacy score of 7.70 with a standard error of 0.62. Participants in the 4+1 year post baccalaureate license only (Path 2) has a mean score of 7.60 with a standard error of 0.68. Participants in the Career

Switchers Alternative Route (Path 5) had a mean score of 7.40 and a standard error of 0.64. Participants in the master of science in education (Path 3) had a mean score of 7.14 with a standard error of 0.80. Participants in the master of science in education for military families (Path 4) had the lowest mean score of 6.32 and a standard error of 0.66.

To compare the overall efficacy of the five license paths' participants, an analysis of variance (ANOVA) was conducted. Results of the one-way analysis of variance indicated a significant difference in overall efficacy scores based upon the five license paths, $F(4,69) = 6.42$, $p = .000$. Table 2.4 describes the multiple comparisons of overall efficacy among the five license paths. The results indicate a statistically significant difference in overall efficacy between the master of science in education for military families ($M = 6.32$) and the IDS + MS (4+1) degree path ($M = 7.70$), $p = .000$, the Career Switchers path ($M = 7.40$), $p = .027$, and the undergraduate+post baccalaureate endorsement path ($M = 7.60$), $p = .002$. The partial eta square for the dependent variable overall efficacy is .271 which is a small effect size.

Table 2.4. Multiple Comparison Tests for Overall Efficacy among the Five License Paths

(I) License Path	(J) License Path	Mean Difference (I–J)	Std. Error	Sig.
IDS 4+1 year MS in Ed	4+1 Post Baccalaureate	.10670	.21149	1.000
	Master of Science in Ed only	.56223	.25604	.315
	MS in Ed for military	1.38341*	.28915	.000
	Career Switchers	.30470	.24400	1.000
4+1 Post Baccalaureate	IDS 4+1 year MS in Ed	–.10670	.21149	1.000
	Master of Science in Ed only	.45553	.29577	1.000
	MS in Ed for military	1.27671*	.32486	.002
	Career Switchers	.19801	.28542	1.000
Master of Science in Ed only	IDS 4+1 year MS in Ed	–.56223	.25604	.315
	4+1 Post Baccalaureate	–.45553	.29577	1.000
	MS in Ed for military	.82118	.35547	.239
	Career Switchers Route	–.25752	.31983	1.000
MS in Ed for military	IDS 4+1 year MS in Ed	–1.38341*	.28915	.000
	4+1 Post Baccalaureate	–1.27671*	.32486	.002
	Master of Science in Ed only	–.82118	.35547	.239
	Career Switchers	–1.07870*	.34691	.027
Career Switchers	IDS 4+1 year MS in Ed	–.30470	.24400	1.000
	4+1 Post Baccalaureate	–.19801	.28542	1.000
	Master of Science in Ed only	.25752	.31983	1.000
	MS in Ed for military families	1.07870*	.34691	.027

Efficacy of Student Engagement

Participants in the IDS 4+1 year master of science in education license path (Path 1) had the highest mean student engagement efficacy score of 7.56 with a standard error of 0.12. Participants in the 4+1 year post baccalaureate license only (Path 2) had a mean score of 7.48 with a standard error of 0.21. Participants in the Career Switchers Alternative Route (Path 5) had a mean score of 7.07 and a standard error of 0.26. Participants in the master of science in education (Path 3) had a mean score of 6.95 with a standard error of 0.27. Participants in the master of science in education for military families (Path 4) had the lowest mean score of 6.29 and a standard error of 0.31.

In order to compare the five license paths' participants' efficacy of student engagement, an analysis of variance (ANOVA) was performed. The results indicated a statistically significant difference between groups in efficacy of student engagement, $F(4,69) = 4.44$, $p = .003$. Table 2.5 displays the analysis

Table 2.5. Multiple Comparison Tests for Efficacy of Student Engagement among the Five License Paths

(I) License Path	(J) License Path	Mean Difference (I–J)	Std. Error	Sig.
IDS 4+1 year MS in Ed	4+1 Post Baccalaureate	.0752	.24619	1.000
	MS in Ed only	.6028	.29805	.470
	MS in Ed for military families	1.2643*	.33659	.004
	Career Switchers	.4865	.28404	.913
4+1 Post Baccalaureate	IDS 4+1 year MS in Ed	–.0752	.24619	1.000
	Master of Science in Ed only	.5276	.34430	1.000
	MS in Ed for military families	1.1891*	.37816	.025
	Career Switchers	.4113	.33225	1.000
Master of Science in Ed only	IDS 4+1 year MS in Ed	–.6028	.29805	.470
	4+1 Post Baccalaureate	–.5276	.34430	1.000
	MS in Ed for military families	.6615	.41380	1.000
	Career Switchers	–.1163	.37231	1.000
MS in Ed for military families	IDS 4+1 year MS in Ed	–1.2643*	.33659	.004
	4+1 Post Baccalaureate	–1.1891*	.37816	.025
	MS in Ed only	–.6615	.41380	1.000
	Career Switchers	–.7778	.40383	.582
Career Switchers	IDS 4+1 year MS in Ed	–.4865	.28404	.913
	4+1 Post Baccalaureate	–.4113	.33225	1.000
	MS in Ed only	.1163	.37231	1.000
	MS in Ed for military families	.7778	.40383	.582

of variance (ANOVA) results for the comparison of mean scores of efficacy of student engagement. Results indicate a statistically significant difference in mean scores between the MS path for military families ($M = 6.29$) and the IDS +MS (4+1) degree ($M = 7.56$), $p = .004$ and the MS path for the military families and the 4+1 post baccalaureate endorsement ($M = 7.48$), p = .025. All other paths did not show a statistically significant difference in efficacy of student engagement with $p > .05$.

Tests of between-subjects effects were performed and determined the partial eta square for the dependent variable efficacy of instructional strategies is .205 which is a small effect size.

Efficacy of Instructional Strategies

For efficacy of instructional strategies, the Career Switchers Alternate Route (Path 5) had the highest mean score of 7.71 with a standard error of 0.25. The IDS 4+1 year master of science in education (Path 1) had the second highest mean score at 7.70 with a standard error of 0.12. The 4+1 year post baccalaureate license only group's (Path 2) mean score was 7.58 with a standard error of 0.21. The master of science in education group's (Path 3) mean score was 7.00 with a standard error of 0.26. The master of science in education for military families (Path 4) had the smallest group's mean of 6.56 with a standard error of 0.30.

In order to compare the five license paths' participants' efficacy of instructional strategies, an analysis of variance (ANOVA) was performed. The results indicated a statistically significant difference between groups $F(4,69) = 4.28$, $p = .004$. Post-hoc tests indicated a statistically significant difference in mean scores between the MS path for military families ($M = 6.56$) and the IDS +MS (4+1) degree ($M = 7.70$), $p = .008$ and the MS path for the military families and Career Switchers Alternative Route participants ($M = 7.71$), $p = .044$. All other paths did not show a statistically significant difference in efficacy of instructional strategies with $p > .05$. The partial eta square for the dependent variable efficacy of instructional strategies .199 which is a small effect size.

Efficacy of Classroom Management

In terms of efficacy of classroom management, The IDS 4+1 year master of science in education group (Path 1) had the highest mean score of 7.85 and a standard error of 0.12. The 4+1 year post baccalaureate license only group (Path 2) had the next largest mean score of 7.73 and a standard error of 0.21. The master of science in education group (Path 3) had a mean score of 7.47

Table 2.6. Multiple Comparison Tests for Efficacy of Instructional Strategies among the Five License Paths

(I) License Path	(J) License Path	Mean Difference (I–J)	Std. Error	Sig.
IDS 4+1 year MS in Ed	4+1 Post Baccalaureate	.1270	.23694	1.000
	Master of Science in Ed only	.7039	.28685	.167
	MS in Ed for military fam.	1.1414*	.32395	.008
	Career Switchers	−.0044	.27337	1.000
4+1 Post Baccalaureate	IDS 4+1 year MS in Ed	−.1270	.23694	1.000
	Master of Science in Ed only	.5769	.33137	.861
	MS in Ed for military fam.	1.0144	.36396	.069
	Career Switchers	−.1314	.31977	1.000
Master of Science in Ed only	IDS 4+1 year MS in Ed	−.7039	.28685	.167
	4+1 Post Baccalaureate	−.5769	.33137	.861
	MS in Ed for military fam.	.4375	.39826	1.000
	Career Switchers	−.7083	.35833	.521
MS in Ed for military fam.	IDS 4+1 year MS in Ed	−1.1414*	.32395	.008
	4+1 Post Baccalaureate	−1.0144	.36396	.069
	Master of Science in Ed only	−.4375	.39826	1.000
	Career Switchers	−1.1458*	.38866	.044
Career Switchers	IDS 4+1 year MS in Ed	.0044	.27337	1.000
	4+1 Post Baccalaureate	.1314	.31977	1.000
	Master of Science in Ed only	.7083	.35833	.521
	MS in Ed for military fam.	1.1458*	.38866	.044

and a standard error of 0.26. The Career Switchers alternative route group (Path 5) had a mean score of 7.42 and a standard error of 0.25. The master of science in education group for military families (Path 4) had the smallest mean score of 6.10 and a standard error of 0.30.

In order to compare the five license paths' participants' efficacy of classroom management, an analysis of variance (ANOVA) was performed. The results indicate a statistically significant difference between groups $F(4,69) = 7.48$, $p=.000$. Results indicate a statistically significant difference in mean scores between the master of science in education path for military families ($M=6.10$) and all four other paths—the Career Switchers ($M=7.42$), $p=.013$, the 4+1 post baccalaureate endorsement ($M=7.73$), $p=.000$, IDS 4+1 year master of science in education. Path ($M=7.85$), $p=.000$, and the master of science in education only ($M=7.47$), $p=.011$.

Table 2.7 indicates a statistically significant difference in efficacy of classroom management between the master of science in education for military families and all other license paths, $p<0.05$. The partial eta square for the dependent variable efficacy of classroom management is .303 which is a moderate effect.

Table 2.7. Multiple Comparisons Tests for Efficacy of Classroom Management among the Five License Paths

License Path (I)	License Path (J)	Mean Difference (I–J)	Std. Error	Sig.
IDS+MS in Ed (4+1)	Post Bach	.1179	.23807	1.000
	MS in Ed	.3799	.29922	1.000
	MS in Ed. military families	1.7445*	.32549	.000
	Career Switchers	.4320	.27467	1.000
Post Bach	IDS + MS in Ed (4+1)	−.1179	.23807	1.000
	MS in Ed.	.2620	.33295	1.000
	MS in Ed military families	1.6266*	.36569	.000
	Career Switchers	.3141	.32129	1.000
MS in Ed	IDS + MS in Ed (4+1)	−.3799	.28822	1.000
	Pos Bach	−.2620	.33295	1.000
	MS in Ed military families	1.3646*	.40015	.011
	Career Switchers	.0521	.36003	1.000
MS in Ed for military families	IDS + MS in Ed (4+1)	−1.7445*	.32549	.000
	Post Bach	−1.6266*	.36569	.000
	MS in Ed	−1.3646*	.40015	.011
	Career Switchers	−1.3125*	.39051	.013
Career Switchers	IDS + MS (4+1)	−.4320	.27467	1.000
	Post Bach	−.3141	.32129	1.000
	MS in Ed	−.0521	.36003	1.000
	MS in Ed military families	1.3125*	.39051	.013

DISCUSSION

Teacher preparation programs strive to implement field experiences that encourage the growth of teacher candidates' efficacy and their commitment to the field of education. The role of formal field experiences has been considered important, however, the variety and length of each formal field experience depended on the requirements of the preparation program's license path and linkages to teacher efficacy were not quantified.

We used Tschannen-Morgan & Woolfolk-Hoy's (2001)'s Teacher Sense of Efficacy Scale questionnaire to determine the amount of influence total hours of field experience had on teacher self-efficacy. Participants' responses from the IDS+MS path (Tiers A, B, C, D, E, F, and G) were analyzed as they experienced larger and larger doses of field experience. The regression analysis indicated a slight, positive correlation between the number of hours of field experiences and overall teacher efficacy. In other words, as students accumulated more hours of field experience, their teaching efficacy increased in a statistically significant manner.

The Teacher Sense of Efficacy Scale questionnaire was also disaggregated into three subscales: efficacy in instructional strategies, efficacy in student engagement, and efficacy in classroom management. Regression analyses determined a slight, yet significant, positive correlation among the hours of formal field experiences with each of the subcategories efficacy of instructional strategies and efficacy in student engagement. The subcategory, efficacy of classroom management had the strongest correlation to number of hours of field experiences. In summary, those who completed more hours of formal field experiences demonstrated more efficacy toward teaching overall and in the specific areas of instructional strategies, student engagement, and classroom management.

Because preparation paths vary widely in the number of hours required for field experiences, we compared the efficacy group means for five license paths' that diverged greatly in required hours. Results indicated a statistically significant difference in the means of the students who completed the MS degree program for military families with each of the other four license paths. This path requires a small field experience (30 hours observation and 10 weeks of student teaching) compared to other paths. Students in the MS path for military families felt less efficacious than those prepared through the IDS + MS, IDS + post baccalaureate endorsement, the master of science in education degree, and the Career Switchers program. It should be noted, however, that this program in its' entirety is very small and the sample size (n=6) for the study reflected the small program size.

DIRECTIONS FOR FURTHER RESEARCH

Teacher candidates' efficacy should be studied further while experiencing varying contextual factors during field experiences. According to Gresham (2008), teaching outcome expectancy is a teacher's belief that successful teaching can bring about student learning despite external factors such as family background, parental influences, and home environment. Siwatu (2011) studied a variety of contextual settings relating to preservice teachers' sense of efficacy with regards to teaching in urban and suburban schools. Results suggest that the contextual factors of the school do matter when relating to teacher efficacy. Many preservice candidates in Siwatu's study felt more prepared to teach in suburban schools compared to in urban schools.

Also, since many students enter their preparation path with preconceived efficacies about teaching particular subjects, it might benefit candidates to determine their most and least confident subjects to teach prior to beginning their coursework. By encouraging self-awareness, candidates can focus on increasing their efficacy levels of the subjects they are not as confident to teach. It would also be valuable to administer the efficacy scale questionnaire to candidates at the beginning of their teacher preparation program and monitor their growth as they complete their required formal field experiences. Further, since candidates' informal field experiences may affect their efficacy levels before they enter a preparation program, questions regarding these informal field experiences should be included in the efficacy scale questionnaire given prior to beginning each preparation program.

Further qualitative research studies would benefit these findings to investigate the specific components about the field experiences that help to increase the teaching efficacy of the future teachers. Determining factors that attribute to preservice teacher efficacy would allow teacher preparation programs and cooperating schools to better understand how to help to increase efficacy of future teachers.

Limitations

Since this study does not focus on specific contextual factors (such as socioeconomic status and other demographic information) affecting teacher candidates' teaching efficacy, findings might be different depending on whether the cooperating schools are in an urban, a rural, or a suburban school environment. Urban and rural schools often present different challenges than those in suburban school settings.

There are a variety of university supervisors and cooperating teachers that are assigned to the different teacher candidates within each license path. Individual opinions about supervisors or cooperating teachers may not accurately represent all university supervisors or cooperating teachers working with the university. Since all of the participants are from the same university, a universal conclusion may not be accurately represented of all teacher preparation programs in the United States. Past informal field experiences may contribute to the increase or lack of efficacy in teaching children prior to enrolling in the preparation program.

Finally, group size among some of the license paths' participants should be noted. Since the participants all came from the same university, many of the paths' sizes had small numbers. Specifically, the path with the least number of participants was the path to have statistically significant differences in efficacy compared to the other paths. The small population may be a limitation to these findings.

CONCLUSIONS

In conclusion, our findings indicate that multiple field experiences are important components of teacher preparation programs. Multiple field experiences provide exposure to real-world classroom teachers, students of a variety of ages and developmental stages, and teaching situations. Our analyses—conducted in two ways—indicated that there is a positive correlation of the number of hours of field experiences to teacher candidates' teaching efficacy. Thus, teacher preparation programs should work toward providing candidates with many hours of authentic field experiences.

REFERENCES

Bandura, A. (1977). *Social learning theory*. New York, NY: General Learning Press.
———. (1993). Perceived self-efficacy in cognitive development and functioning. *Educational Psychologist, 28*(2), 117–148.
———. (1997). *Self-efficacy: The exercise of control*. New York, NY: W. H. Freeman.
Berry, B., Daughtery, A., & Wieder, A. (2010). *Teacher leadership: Leading the way to effective teaching and learning*. Center for Teaching Quality, 1–20. Retrieved from files.eric.ed.gov/fulltext/ED509719.pdf
Boyd, D., Grossman, P., Lankford, H., Loeb, S., & Wyckoff, J. (2008). *Teacher preparation and student achievement*. Calder Working Paper No. 20. Washington, DC: National Center for Analysis of Longitudinal Data in Education Research.
Bruce, C., & Ross, J. (2008). A model for increasing reform implementation and teacher efficacy: Teacher peer coaching in grades 3 and 6 mathematics. *Canadian Journal of Education, 31*(2), 346–370.
Clift, R., & Brady, P. (2005). Research on methods courses and field experiences. In M. Cochran-Smith & K. Zeichner (Eds.), *Studying teacher education: The report of the AERA panel on research and teacher education* (pp. 309–424). Mahwah, NJ: American Educational Research Association.
Erawan, P. (2011). A path analysis for factors affecting pre-service teachers' teaching efficacy. *American Journal of Scientific Research, 13*, 47–58.
Glenn, G., Meyers, L. Guarino, A. (2008). *Analysis of variance designs: A conceptual and computational approach with SPSS and SAS*. New York, NY: Cambridge University Press.

Goddard, R., Hoy, W., & Hoy, A. (2000). Collective teacher efficacy: Its meaning, measure, and impact on student achievement. *American Educational Research Journal, 37*(2), 479–507.

Gresham, G. (2008). Mathematics anxiety and mathematics teacher efficacy in elementary pre-service teachers. *Teaching Education, 19* (3), 171–184.

Gurvitch, R., & Metzler, M. (2009). The effects of laboratory-based and field-based practicum experience on pre-service teachers' self-efficacy. *Teaching and Teacher Education, 25,* 437–443.

Liaw, E. C. (2009). Teacher efficacy of pre-service teachers in Taiwan: The influence of classroom teaching and group discussions. *Teaching and Teacher Education, 25*(1), 176–180.

Siwatu, K. O. (2011). Pre-service teachers' sense of preparedness and self-efficacy to teach in America's urban and suburban schools: Does context matter? *Teaching and Teacher Education, 27,* 357–365.

Swars, S. L. (2005). Examining perceptions of mathematics teaching effectiveness among elementary preservice teachers with differing levels of mathematics teacher efficacy. *Journal of Instructional Psychology, 32*(2), 139–147.

Tschannen-Moran, M., & Anita Woolfolk Hoy (2001). Teacher efficacy: Capturing and elusive construct. *Teaching and Teacher Education, 17,* 783–805.

———. (2007). The differential antecedents of self-efficacy beliefs of novice and experienced teachers. *Teaching and Teacher Education, 23*(6), 944–956.

Tuchman, E., & Isaacs, J. (2011). The influence of formal and informal formative pre-service experiences on teacher self-efficacy. *Educational Psychology, 31*(4), 413–433.

Chapter Three

How Reflectivity Impacts Teacher Candidates' Self-efficacy

Sherri M. Weber and Julie J. Henry

John F. Kennedy warned, "The course of civilization is a race between catastrophe and education. In a democracy such as ours, we must make sure that education wins the race" (Peters & Woolley, 2017). Educators are key to the preservation of civilization; however, in today's climate of accountability, it is increasingly challenging for young people to become teachers (Parkay, Stanford, & Gougeon, 2010) and to maintain the professional confidence and commitment to enter the profession.

Teacher educators need to consider new ways to foster the self-confidence of teacher candidates so that they persist in developing their teaching skills and are successful in the standardized assessments required for certification. The purpose of this study was to investigate how videotaping may affect the self-efficacy of teacher candidates and the impact it may have on teacher candidates' confidence in completing the videotape portion of the educative Teacher Performance Assessment (edTPA™) which is required for program completion and/or certification in several states (SCALE, 2016).

REVIEW OF RESEARCH

Teacher self-efficacy has been found to predict teachers' use of teaching strategies, the motivation and achievement of their students, and the likelihood that teachers will stay in the teaching profession (Skaalvik & Skaalvik, 2007). The concept of self-efficacy comes from social cognitive theory, which situates learning within a social context with a dynamic and reciprocal interaction of the person, environment, and behavior.

Bandura defined self-efficacy as "people's judgments of their capabilities to organize and execute courses of action required to attain designated types of performance" (Bandura 1986, p. 391). Self-efficacy is a belief about what an individual can accomplish in a specific context (Zimmerman & Cleary, 2006). Social cognitive theories have described how people set goals and anticipate likely outcomes and how effort and perseverance are related to this construct (Pajares, 1997).

Teacher self-efficacy refers to teachers' beliefs about their ability to plan and implement activities required to influence student outcomes (Wheatley, 2005). Researchers have identified different dimensions of self-efficacy including confidence in the areas of instructional strategies, classroom management, and student engagement (Tschannen-Moran & Woolfolk Hoy, 2001) adapting education to individual student's needs, motivating students, cooperating with colleagues and parents, and coping with changes and challenges (Skaalvik & Skaalvik, 2007).

Researchers have found that self-efficacy can be enhanced through mastery experiences, where the individual interprets his or her performance as successful (Bong & Skaalvik, 2003). This is particularly effective when individuals are uncertain of their own abilities (Schunk, 1987). Social cognitive theory emphasizes that people are self-regulating and self-reflecting and that reflection about mastery experiences can impact self-efficacy.

Videotaping has been found to be a stimulus for reflectivity in teacher candidates. Recording themselves teaching lessons for self-observation helps them to notice and respond to strengths and weaknesses in their teaching (Hetzner & Vevea, 2010: Orlova, 2009). Video can be examined multiple times and by multiple viewers and can be a catalyst for learning about teaching (Huston, 2016).

Videotaping in teacher education programs can fill two roles; it is an opportunity for reflection and an opportunity to present performance evidence to demonstrate competency. The implementation of the educative Teacher Performance Assessment (edTPA™), which includes videotaped performance and is a requirement for program completion or for certification in many states, has stimulated new interest in incorporating videotaping as a tool to demonstrate both competence and reflectivity.

Videotaping and edTPA™

The Stanford Center for Assessment, Learning and Equity (SCALE, 2016), in partnership with the American Association of Colleges for Teacher Education (AACTE, 2017) developed the edTPA™ to measure teacher candidates' readiness to teach. The edTPA™ is the first nationally available, educator-designed performance assessment for teachers entering the profession (SCALE, 2016). The assessment was designed to improve the assessment of teacher candidates and ultimately reform and distinguish teaching as a profession. It was expected that candidates who scored well on edTPA™ would be more likely to be effective teachers in the future.

The edTPA™ also was developed to allow teacher preparation programs the opportunity to assess program effectiveness. Some teacher education leaders were optimistic about the development of a standardized performance assessment that included authentic tasks to use for teacher candidate performance and teacher preparation program review, noting that "by evaluating teaching authentically, they (performance assessments) represent the complexity of teaching and offer standards that can define an expert profession" (Darling-Hammond & Hyler, 2013, p. 13).

In 2017, it was reported that eighteen states had either adopted statewide policies requiring a performance assessment for aspiring teachers or were actively considering such a step and that 765 educator preparation programs were using edTPA™ across forty states (AACTE, 2017) The edTPA™ website stated that the long-term expectation was that institutions of higher education and/or state education boards throughout the United States would be adopting edTPA™ as a requirement for an education degree and/or for teacher licensure (http://edTPA™.aacte.org/state-policy).

SCALE (2016) reports that the edTPA™ drew on experience gained from other performance-based assessments of teaching, including the National Board for Professional Teaching Standards and the Performance Assessment for California Teachers (PACT) (edTPA™, 2016). The edTPA™ has been developed in twenty-seven different fields based on licensure areas. This comprehensive assessment includes artifacts (including fifteen to twenty minutes of videotaped instruction) demonstrating candidates' abilities to plan, instruct, and assess particular learning segments of three to five lessons during student teaching. The three tasks (planning, instructing, and assessing) allow candidate work to be scored using a series of fifteen rubrics, five rubrics per task for most versions.

The rubrics are based on a 5-point score, 1–5, which rates candidates' work along a continuum from not ready to teach (depicted by a teacher-focused, whole-class, fragmented or indiscriminate presentation of work) scored as a 1, to a highly accomplished beginner teacher (evidence of student-focused, individual or flexible groups, integrated, intentional, and well executed presentation of work) scored as a 5. Teacher preparation programs have been offering opportunities for candidates to practice parts of the edTPA™ within the preparation program in order to assist candidates in meeting this new requirement and demonstrating their readiness for teaching.

RESEARCH DESIGN

The purpose of this research was to examine the effectiveness of the completion of a videotape project in a literacy methods class that was designed to be a parallel task for the video portion of the edTPA™. This was a mixed methods study using a Likert-type survey given pre- and post-assessment to an experimental and control group. In addition, the experimental group completed an open-ended survey about their experiences using the video. This research design was selected as the most effective way to gather data to answer the research questions.

The video project required students to videotape themselves teaching a literacy lesson in an elementary classroom, edit it down to twenty minutes and write a reflection following many of the guidelines and prompts from the video portion of the edTPA™. The assignment appears in appendix A.

The research questions guiding this investigation were as follows:

- How does the video reflection assignment affect teacher self-efficacy for teacher candidates?
- How does the video reflection assignment affect confidence for edTPA™?

Context and Participants

Teacher candidates at a large, public urban comprehensive college completed a six-credit course in literacy methods during their junior year. The course included a forty-hour field experience where they observed instruction, assisted the classroom teacher, and taught at least three whole-class literacy lessons. In addition, for this investigation, fourteen teacher candidates completed the video reflection assignment with one professor (intervention group), and twenty teacher candidates (in two sections) completed their practicum with another professor without including this assignment (comparison group).

The intervention group received instruction about how to complete the videotaping and how to interpret the reflective prompts. These participants were given access to video equipment available in the college library. This was a convenience sample of participants who were enrolled for different sections of this course. All participants completed a consent form, and the research design was approved by the campus Institutional Review Board (IRB).

Data Sources and Analysis

All participants completed a quantitative survey pre and post (appendix B). In addition, the intervention group completed a qualitative survey (appendix C) at the end of the semester. The quantitative survey contained fifteen Likert-style items. Twelve items were adapted from items in a teacher-efficacy scale related to instruction, adapting instruction for individual needs, and motivating students (Skaalvik & Skaalvik, 2007). The final three items were designed by the researchers to measure the effectiveness of completing the video project intervention in preparing for edTPA™. The qualitative survey was designed by the researchers to elicit open-ended responses to gather more information about how the video assignment impacted their confidence as developing teachers and how the assignment impacted their preparedness for the edTPA™.

Quantitative data were entered into SPSS software. Self-efficacy scores pre and post were calculated for each group based on the mean scores for items 1–12. An analysis of variance was used to determine if the differences between groups for increases in self-efficacy were statistically significant. Video reflectivity scores were calculated for each group based on items 13–15, and post-test means were compared using a two sample t-test.

Narrative analysis was used to interpret the qualitative comments from participants in order to co-construct meaning between the researchers and participants (Etherington & Bridges, 2011). This approach reflects the perspective that meaning is best captured through the qualitative nuances of the participants' ordinary language (Polkinghorne, 1988).

FINDINGS

Data from the quantitative survey were used to answer the research questions about how the video reflection assignment affected teacher self-efficacy and confidence for edTPA™. Narrative analysis was used to reveal the personal understandings of the participants and how the stories made sense together. These data will be presented for each research question below.

Research Question 1: How does the video reflection assignment affect teacher self-efficacy for teacher candidates?

Both groups completed the quantitative assessment of self-efficacy at the beginning and end of the semester. Figure 3.1 shows the pre and post scores for each group. The intervention group showed gains in self-efficacy from a mean of 4.26 to 5.89. The comparison group showed gains in self-efficacy from a mean of 5.14 to 5.59. Self-efficacy gain scores (posttest-pretest) were analyzed in an analysis of variance with intervention group (intervention vs. comparison) as the independent variable. The increase in self-efficacy was greater for participants in the intervention group ($M = 19.00$) than for those in the comparison group ($M = 6.40$), $F(1, 31) = 8.12$. The difference in gains between the two groups was statistically significant $(p < .01)$.

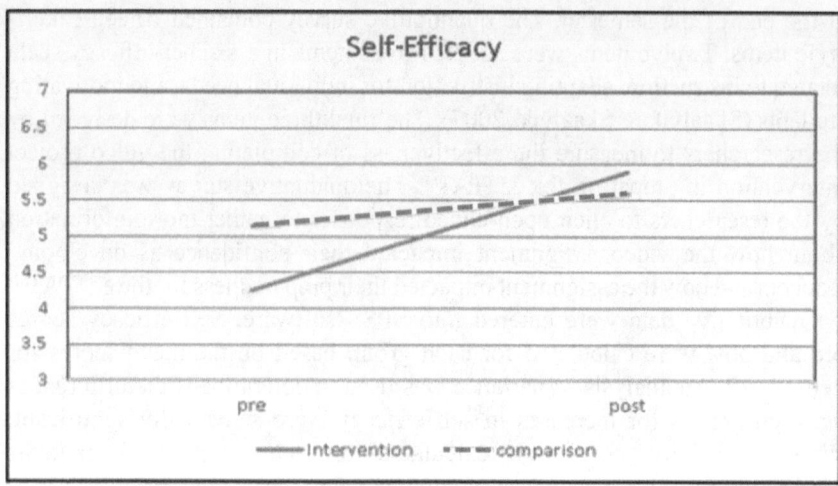

Figure 3.1. Self-efficacy scores.
This figure shows mean scores from the self-efficacy measure for intervention group and comparison group at the beginning and end of the semester. Author created: Author confirmation via phone call 10/18/19.

Comments from the qualitative survey indicated that teacher candidates found the video assignment helpful in viewing themselves as teachers and in reflecting on their teaching. While reading the comments, researchers took in what was being said and compared it with our personal understandings of the students' experiences and came to know more about how videotaping helped them to view themselves as competent teachers. This was evident when Megan shared, "I was able to see my teacher role. It was nice to see how my switch goes on when I teach; it's like being another person." Megan's response demonstrates that she has gained self-confidence in her teaching by seeing herself in this role through the review of the video. Sara revealed a similar narrative when she described her growing self-confidence when she watched the video of herself teaching and exclaimed, "I actually looked like a teacher!"

Candidates also were able to use the videos as reflective tools. Kate was able to watch and rewatch herself in the video, which helped her to identify and appreciate all of the little nuances of her teaching so that she could critique herself and continue to grow as a teacher. This was also evident when Susan was able to use the video to see and hear herself in the classroom and use this to reflect on what was effective or ineffective in her interactions. She explained, "Watching myself teach, listening to how I talk and move around . . . it's like a whole different perspective! When I got to go back and watch myself speak, I noticed things about myself I never noticed before." These stories illustrate how video has an impact on students' ability to physically look back and reflect on their performance.

Table 3.1. Analysis of Video Reflection Scores

	Video Reflectivity Scores Intervention Group Mean N=14	Video Reflectivity Scores Comparison Group Mean N=20
Pre	4.74	4.71
Post	6.36	5.33
Gain Scores	1.62	.62*

Research Question 2: How does the video reflection assignment affect confidence for edTPA™?

The video reflection scores were also analyzed. The groups started with similar response scores (intervention group, $M = 4.74$ and comparison group $M = 4.71$) (see table 3.1). The intervention group showed gains of 1.62, whereas the comparison group showed a gain of only .62. A two sample t-test found that the post-test video reflection scores for the intervention group were significantly greater than those of the comparison group, $t = 3.85, p < .0001$.

When they were specifically asked about how the video assignment impacted their preparedness for edTPA™, certain stories were able to reveal more common interpretations. Megan's experiences left her feeling "prepared and confident to complete the edTPA™ tasks in the future." Sara also was able to find confidence from the preparation she received doing the practice edTPA™. She revealed, "I know what to expect now. I won't be as nervous doing the real edTPA™." These stories, in fact, illustrate the impact that practice edTPA™ tasks can have on teacher candidates' confidence and self-efficacy.

CONCLUSIONS

The focus of this investigation was to examine the effectiveness of completing a videotape project in a literacy methods class that was designed to be a parallel task for the video portion of the edTPA™. The researchers sought to determine if the video reflection assignment affected teacher candidates' self-efficacy. Did they view themselves in a more positive manner after watching themselves on video? Analyses revealed that the intervention group showed a significant increase in their self-efficacy scores. Researchers also examined if the video reflection assignment affected confidence in responding to the prompts in the reflective piece of the edTPA™. Did the teacher candidates feel more prepared and confident after completing the parallel task for the video portion of the edTPA™?

Video reflectivity scores indicated that teacher candidates found the video assignment helpful and impacted their preparedness for the edTPA™. Teacher candidates reported feeling not only prepared and confident, but could see themselves in a teacher role, giving them a whole different perspective than a supervisor telling them what they did right and wrong. Both videotaping and completing the video assignment appeared to help teacher candidates to feel more self-assured and equipped in completing the edTPA™.

It may be beneficial for teacher preparation programs to provide an opportunity for teacher candidates to practice videotaping and reflecting on their teaching. Having teacher candidates critique and reflect on their teaching via videotaping can be a powerful experience and provide a new prospective for the teacher candidate as well as the instructor, while enhancing the self-efficacy and confidence for teacher candidates.

This may provide significant benefits for the field as research has shown that teacher self-efficacy is related to good teaching, the motivation and achievement of students in the classroom, and the likelihood that teachers will stay in the teaching profession (Skaalvik & Skaalvik, 2007). In this way, we can equip teacher candidates with the tools and confidence to become successful teaching professionals.

APPENDIX A

Videotaping Project: Instructing and Engaging Students in Learning

You will hand in a jump drive containing 1–2 video clips (together totaling no more than twenty minutes) that demonstrate how you interact with students in a positive literacy environment to develop an essential literacy strategy and to support students to independently apply the essential literacy strategy to comprehend or compose text. This can be connected to comprehension, vocabulary development, word study/phonics, fluency, or writing. You can feature the whole class or a targeted group of students within the class. Each video clip must be continuous and unedited, with no interruption.

Instruction Commentary (5–10 pages, double spaced, excluding lesson plan)

1. Promoting a Positive Learning Environment:
   Identify scenes in the video using timestamps where you provided a positive learning environment. How did you demonstrate respect for, rapport with, and responsiveness to students with varied needs and diverse backgrounds? If you did not do this, describe how you could do this next time you video.
2. Engaging Students in Learning:
   Using timestamps. refer to examples from the clips in your explanations. Explain how your instruction engaged students in learning the literacy strategy and skills. Describe how your instruction linked with prior learning and personal, cultural, and community assets. If you did not do this, describe how you could do this the next time you video.
3. Deepening Student Learning during Instruction
   Using timestamps, refer to examples from the clips in your explanations. Explain how you prompted student responses to encourage thinking. Explain how you supported students to apply the literacy strategy in a meaningful context including opportunities for guided practice. If you did not do this, describe how you could do this next time.
4. Analyzing Teaching Effectiveness
   - Using timestamps, refer to examples from the clips in your explanations. How did your instruction support learning for the whole class, including struggling learners and learners who may need more challenge?
   - What changes would you make to your instruction to better support student learning for the whole class and varied learners? Why do you think these changes would improve student learning? Use theory and research to support your reasoning and include at least two references in APA format.

APPENDIX B

Please circle the number below that best expresses your certainty about each statement.

	1	2	3	4	5	6	7
	Not certain at all			Neutral			Absolutely certain
How certain are you that you can . . .	1	2	3	4	5	6	7
1. Explain central themes in literacy so that even the low-achieving students understand.	1	2	3	4	5	6	7
2. Get all students in class to work hard with their schoolwork.	1	2	3	4	5	6	7
3. Organize schoolwork to adapt instruction and assignments to individual needs.	1	2	3	4	5	6	7
4. Provide good guidance and instruction to all students regardless of their level of ability.	1	2	3	4	5	6	7
5. Wake the desire to learn even among the lowest-achieving students.	1	2	3	4	5	6	7
6. Provide realistic challenge for all students even in mixed-ability classes.	1	2	3	4	5	6	7
7. Answer students' questions so that they understand difficult work.	1	2	3	4	5	6	7
8. Get students to do their best even when working with difficult work.	1	2	3	4	5	6	7
9. Explain subject matter so that most students understand the basic principles.	1	2	3	4	5	6	7

10. Adapt instruction to the needs of low-ability students while also attending to the needs of other students in the class.	1	2	3	4	5	6	7
11. Motivate students who show low interest in schoolwork.	1	2	3	4	5	6	7
12. Organize classroom work so that both low- and high-ability students work with tasks that are adapted to their abilities.	1	2	3	4	5	6	7
13. Complete the video requirements for the edTPA.	1	2	3	4	5	6	7
14. Watch video and use it to reflect on my teaching.	1	2	3	4	5	6	7
15. Choose segments from video to document my teaching effectiveness.	1	2	3	4	5	6	7

APPENDIX C

Feedback about the Video Assignment

Please answer the questions below:

1. How did the video assignment impact your confidence as a developing teacher?
2. What part of the video assignment was most informative for you?
3. How did the video assignment impact your confidence regarding your preparedness for the edTPA™?

REFERENCES

AACTE. (2017). *edTPA™*. Retrieved from http://edTPA™.aacte.org/faq#58.

Bandura, A. (1986) *Social foundations of thought and action: A social cognitive theory.* New York, NY: Freeman.

Bong, M., & Skaalvik, E. (2003). Academic self-concept and self-efficacy: How different are they really? *Educational Psychology Review, 15*, 1–40.

Darling-Hammond, L., & Hyler, M. (2013). The role of performance assessment in developing teaching as a profession. *Rethinking Schools, 27*, 10–15.

edTPA™ (2016). *Educative Assessment and Meaningful Support 2016 edTPA Administrative Report*. Retrieved from https://secure.aacte.org/apps/rl/resource.php?resid=647&ref=edtpa.

Etherington, K., & Bridges, N. (2011). Narrative case study research: On endings and six session Reviews. *Counselling and Psychotherapy Research, 11*(1), 11–22.

Hetzner, A., & Vevea, B. (2010, December 5). Building a better teacher: How to best educate future teachers. *Milwaukee-Wisconsin Journal Sentinel*. Retrieved from http://www.jsonline.com/news/education/111329924.html

Huston, T. (2016). How edTPA™ may help pre-service teachers understand children. *Teacher Education and Practice, 29*, 152–172.

Orlova, N. (2009). Video Recording as a Stimulus for Reflection in Pre-Service EFL Teacher Training. *English Teaching Forum, 47*(2). 30–35.

Pajares, F. (1997). Current directions in self-efficacy research. In H. W. Marsh, R. G. Craven, and D. M. McInerney (Eds.), *International advances in self research* (pp. 1–49). Greenwich, CT: Information Age.

Parkay, F. W., Stanford, B. H., & Gougeon, T. D. (2010). *Becoming a teacher* (8th Edition). Boston, MA: Pearson/Merrill.

Peters, G., & Woolley, J. (2017). *The American Presidency Project*. Retrieved from http://www.presidency.ucsb.edu/ws/?pid=74293

Polkinghorne, D. (1988). *Narrative knowing and the human sciences*. Albany, NY: State University of New York Press.

Schunk, D. (1987). Peer models and children's behavioral change. *Review of Educational Research, 57*, 149–174.

Skaalvik, E., & Skaalvik, S. (2007). Dimensions of teacher self-efficacy and relations with strain factors, perceived collective teacher efficacy and teacher burnout. *Journal of Educational Psychology, 99*, 3, 611–625.

Stanford Center for Assessment, Learning and Equity (SCALE). (2016). *edTPA™*. Palo Alto, CA: Author. Retrieved from https://scale.stanford.edu/teaching/edTPA™.

Tschannen-Moran, M. & Anita Woolfolk Hoy (2001). Teacher efficacy: Capturing an elusive construct. *Teaching and Teacher Education, 17*, 783–805.

Wheatley, K. (2005). The case for reconceptualizing teacher efficacy research. *Teaching and Teacher Education, 21*, 747–766.

Zimmerman, B. J., & Cleary, T. J. (2006). Adolescents' development of personal agency. In F. Pajares, & T. Urdan (Eds.), *Adolescence and Education (Vol. 5): Self-Efficacy Beliefs of Adolescents* (pp. 45–69). Greenwich, CT: Information Age Publishing.

Chapter Four

A Framework for Measuring Algebra Teacher Self-efficacy

Trena L. Wilkerson, M. Alejandra Sorto,
William A. Jasper, Sandra Cooper, Winifred Mallam,
Colleen M. Eddy, Yolanda A. Parker,
Sarah Quebec Fuentes, Judy M. Taylor,
and Elizabeth K. Ward

Internationally, algebra has been seen as an essential curriculum element (Leung, Park, Holton, & Clarke, 2014; Norris, 2012). In particular, algebra has been identified as a predictor of academic success in college and future employment earnings in the United States (Adelman, 2006; National Mathematics Advisory Panel, 2008). Therefore, developing algebra teachers who are confident and competent in their abilities to teach algebra is essential. A team of mathematics educators from nine universities/colleges in south-central United States collaborated to develop a framework for examining algebra teacher self-efficacy.

This chapter describes the process of the development of the framework that could lead to survey instruments or evaluation/assessment protocols that will measure teachers' self-efficacy in teaching algebra. At present, there are instruments available to measure efficacious behaviors such as student self-efficacy, teacher self-efficacy, and mathematics and science elementary teacher self-efficacy. Recently an instrument was validated related to measuring teachers' self-efficacy to teach middle grades statistics (Harrell-Williams et al., 2014). So, while there is a movement to develop more specific instruments to measure self-efficacy in teaching, there is none specific to the content area of algebra.

There is a need for domain-specific frameworks and measures of teacher efficacy as called for by efficacy researchers such as Bandura (1997) and Pajares (1996). Pajares stated "omnibus tests that aim to assess general self-efficacy provide global scores that decontextualize the self-efficacy-behavior correspondence and transform self-efficacy beliefs into a generalized personality trait rather than the context-specific judgment Bandura suggests they are" (Pajares, 1996, p. 547). At the initial stages of this project, it was critical to develop a strong framework that could lead to a foundation for assessing the algebra teacher self-efficacy construct.

Prior to developing research and assessment tools to measure teacher self-efficacy in algebra, it was prudent to ensure that the appropriate aspects of algebra content and pedagogy were both addressed. This chapter presents such a framework for measuring algebra teacher self-efficacy that is grounded in theory and curricular documents.

We begin by addressing why algebra was targeted and the implications related to teaching algebra followed by a discussion of teacher efficacy as a construct and measurement approach. For a complete account of the historical development of research on teacher efficacy and the development of related instruments see Henson's (2002) article in *Educational Psychologist*; Tschannen-Moran, Woolfolk-Hoy, and Hoy's (1998) work; or Akbari and Tavassoli's (2014) discussion. The remainder of this paper describes the process followed by the researchers to develop a framework for algebra teacher self-efficacy.

WHY ALGEBRA?

There is a consensus both internationally (Leung et al., 2014; Norris, 2012; Royal Society, 2011) and in U.S. educational policy that students should have access to algebra (Stein, Kaufman, Sherman, & Hillen, 2011). The specifics related to the focus may vary from country to country. The United States' *Common Core State Standards for Mathematics* (CCSS-M), adopted by forty-two out of the fifty states, District of Columbia, U.S. Virgin Islands, American Samoa, Guam, and Northern Mariana Islands (http://www.core standards.org/standards-in-your-state/; retrieved January 15, 2016), state that students should have access to algebra in eighth grade (National Governors Association [NGA] & Center for Best Practices and Council of Chief State School Officers [CCSSO], 2010). In addition, algebra is viewed as the gateway to higher education in the United States and necessary for the workforce calling for all students across grade levels to be prepared to take algebra and engage in algebraic thinking (Kaput, 2000; Moses, 1995; Moses & Cobb, 2001; NGA & CCSSO, 2010).

There are several common factors that have been used to justify the argument that all students should study algebra: (1) global competitiveness (Leung et al., 2014; National Commission on Excellence in Education [NCEE], 1983; Royal Society, 2011; Schoenfeld, 2004), (2) equitable opportunities for students (National Council of Teachers of Mathematics [NCTM], 2000; National Research Council [NRC], 1989; RAND Mathematics Study Panel, 2003), (3) the incorporation of algebraic thinking in the

K–12 mathematics curriculum (Kaput, 2000; National Council of Teachers of Mathematics Commission on Standards for School, 1989; NCTM, 2000; NGA & CCSSO, 2010), and (4) high-stakes assessments (Chazan, 2008; No Child Left Behind [NCLB], 2001).

Furthermore, "Algebra occupies a special place among the various domains (of mathematics) because it is more than a topical domain. It provides linguistic and representative tools for work throughout mathematics" (RAND Mathematics Study Panel, 2003, p. 48).

There is specific attention on the lack of proficiency of students in the United States in algebra and concern over the lack of a sufficient number of qualified teachers in mathematics (Moses & Cobb, 2001; National Science Foundation, 2009). These factors place schools and teacher education institutions in a critical position. There is a demand for more students to take algebra and be successful in high school as preparation for higher education. Bailey (2009) reported how large numbers of students taking remedial courses in mathematics at the college level lack preparedness for the rigors of college. The number of underprepared and unqualified teachers, that is those teaching out of their field in mathematics, compounds the problem (NCLB, 2001; NRC, 2010, 2011; Ringrose & Adkison, 2009).

Ingersoll and Perda (2010) noted that during the 1999–2000 school year when hiring problems were at a twenty-year high, about 31 percent of secondary schools in their study reported major difficulties finding qualified teachers to fill openings in mathematics and science. This is particularly significant in high-poverty, urban school districts, and rural areas in the United States, which often cannot compete with suburban districts for adequately trained teachers and where teacher retention rates are low (Ingersoll, 2004). Stein et al. (2011, p. 454) also stated,

> [T]he imposition of a mandate for universal algebra necessarily leads to additional challenges such as the need for more teachers to accommodate the larger numbers of students in algebra and for new ways to deal with greater heterogeneity of the students who compose algebra enrollments.

These changes, in turn, create new contexts for student learning.

Thus, more students are taking algebra, and their teachers are not always fully qualified, especially in high-needs school districts.

IMPLICATIONS FOR TEACHING ALGEBRA

Teacher perceptions about algebra and teaching algebra most often begin with their own personal experience as a student. However, the foundation for transitioning from a student to a teacher begins with their teacher preparation. In a study to examine preservice teachers' perceptions of algebra, Bishop and Stump (2000) found that overall many did not understand the distinction between arithmetic and algebra, and even for those that were able to make the distinction, a majority held a procedural perspective.

Stephens (2008) learned that preservice teachers have narrow conceptions of algebra that focused on the use of symbols and manipulation of those symbols. In this study of thirty preservice teachers, Stephens determined that when asked to identify tasks as algebra or non-algebra, most often the preservice teachers labeled tasks as algebra simply because it included a variable or letter.

Schmidt and Bednarz (1997) reported that preservice teachers had the perception that algebra was difficult and identified it as an obscure system based on arbitrary rules. In an attempt to further extend this research with their own study, Van Dooren, Verschaffel, and Onghena (2002) found that secondary preservice teachers in their study elected to use algebraic procedures as their problem-solving preference, even for problems that could be solved arithmetically. With these dominant perceptions about algebra, preservice teachers may have formed a framework for learning to teach algebra that is based on the same procedural notions.

Brown, Davis, and Kulm (2011) conducted a study with twenty-one preservice teachers seeking middle level certification to learn more about their knowledge for teaching algebra for equity. One result from this study was that a majority of the participants held the belief that they understood the math concepts well enough to teach them; however, more than half of these preservice teachers were not able to answer the mathematics problems given to them correctly. The procedural perceptions preservice teachers have about algebra and a possible disconnect between knowledge for teaching and actual content knowledge may potentially lead to instructional issues in the classroom. This suggests that there are two different but related aspects when it comes to teaching algebra.

While there has been a major focus on algebra standards for students in the United States (NGA & CCSSO, 2010), there has been limited attention on the content knowledge and instructional strategies teachers must possess to help all students be successful in algebra. Research studies that have analyzed instructional strategies of teachers, often through surveys, have usually been general in application and not specific to the content the teacher is addressing (Balfanz, Legters, & Jordan, 2004; Ham & Walker, 1999; Williams, Haertel, & Kirst, 2011). Examples of items include *use of cooperative learning strategies* (Balfanz et al., 2004) and *use of graphing calculators* (Ham & Walker, 1999).

These teacher surveys do not specifically align with the content and skills that are required of students in algebra. A more specific instrument was recently developed by a team of researchers (Reckase, McCrory, Floden, Ferrini-Mundy, & Senk, 2015), which is intended to measure three types of secondary mathematics teacher knowledge: knowledge of school mathematics, knowledge of advanced mathematics, and knowledge of mathematics specific to teaching around algebra.

Several reasons exist why algebra should be a focus for mathematics teachers. One is the current advancement in technology that allows the arithmetic to be solved, but the user must have the algebraic thinking so the arithmetic can be solved continuously (Devlin, 2009). Another reason is the idea that algebra is the gateway to college in the United States, which in addition to educational attainment, leads to economic access (Moses & Cobb, 2001; National Academy of Sciences, National Academy of Engineering & Institute of Medicine, 2007; NRC, 2011).

A teacher's belief that all students can handle the rigor of algebra is important for various ethnicity groups and students from low SES backgrounds who have been underrepresented in advanced mathematics courses (College Board, 2000; Davenport et al., 1998). Student success in algebra leads to doors opening for success in higher-level mathematics in high school, college and careers, especially those that are becoming increasingly technological (American Diploma Project, 2004; RAND Mathematics Study Panel, 2003; Texas Education Agency [TEA], 2009).

As noted by the National Mathematics Advisory Panel (2008), "a strong grounding in high school mathematics through Algebra II or higher correlates powerfully with access to college, graduation from college, and earning in the top quartile of income from employment" (p. xii). This underscores the need for teachers to have strong algebraic content knowledge as well as the ability and confidence to teach algebra.

TEACHER EFFICACY

A major focus of education research during the last twenty-five years has been teachers and their effectiveness. John Goodlad's 1984 study of schools identified the teacher as a major factor in the schooling process and emphasized a critical need to examine teachers' beliefs. In particular, there is a need to investigate both inservice and preservice teachers' beliefs concerning teaching and how these beliefs initially form and then change with time and experiences (White, 2000).

Teachers' belief patterns dealing with what they can attain in their classroom and their effectiveness have been termed teacher efficacy. From this point on in this paper the term *teacher efficacy* will be used to refer to the field of study (Henson, 2002). According to Tschannen-Moran and Woolfolk-Hoy (2001), teacher efficacy is a teacher's "judgment of his or her capabilities to bring about desired outcomes of student engagement and learning, even among those students who may be difficult or unmotivated" (p. 783).

Many researchers have contributed to teacher efficacy (e.g., Allinder, 1994; Ashton, 1984; Ashton, Webb, & Doda, 1983; Berman, McLaughlin, Bass, Pauly, & Zellman, 1977; Dellinger, Bobbett, Oliver, & Ellett, 2008; Evans & Tribble, 1986; Gibson & Dembo, 1984; Glickman & Tamashiro, 1982; Goddard, Hoy, & Woolfolk, 2000; Gorrell & Capron, 1989; Guskey, 1984, 1988; Ward, 2009; Wilkerson, 1996; Woolfolk & Hoy, 1990). It is Bandura's (1977) work with self-efficacy that is referred to most often when investigating the link between levels of efficacy and teaching. Bandura (1997) emphasizes the influence of teacher's perceived self-efficacy on students and the classroom stating

> Teachers who have a high sense of instructional efficacy devote more classroom time to academic activities, provide students who encounter difficulties with the guidance they need to succeed, and praise their academic accomplishments. In contrast, teachers of low perceived efficacy spend more time on nonacademic pastimes, readily give up on students if they do not get quick results, and criticize them for their failures. (p. 241)

Gibson and Dembo (1984) found that teachers' levels of instructional efficacy did indeed influence the types of learning experiences they created for their students. More recently Ross (2014) found that there was a connection in levels of self-efficacy among mathematics teachers in relation to working with English Language Learners in the United States.

While teachers do need deep mathematical content knowledge and particular understandings in mathematical pedagogical knowledge, they also need a strong belief in what they can do as teachers of mathematics, having confidence in their ability to reach all students and assist them in being successful in mathematics; that is, a sense of self-efficacy. Ball, Thames, and Phelps (2008) noted how research on pedagogical content knowledge has lacked focus including the relationship to teacher beliefs.

Enochs, Smith, and Huinker (2000) noted an inconsistency in the research on teacher preparation dealing with beliefs of preservice teachers further underlining that both content knowledge and teacher beliefs are important in teacher preparation and should be addressed. In the recent construct validation for the Self-Efficacy Teaching and Knowledge Instrument for Science

Teachers (SETAKIST) (Roberts & Henson, 2000) and the revised version (Pruski et al., 2013), two dimensions were identified: knowledge and teaching self-efficacies. This further underscores the potential need for examining both content knowledge and teaching beliefs.

Woolfolk-Hoy, Davis, and Pape (2006) and Woolfolk and Hoy (1990) noted that teachers' sense of self-efficacy is one of the few teacher characteristics that has been consistently linked to students' behavior and learning. Teachers' self-efficacy is a crucial component in students' achievement (Armor et al., 1976; Ashton & Webb, 1986; Bandura 1997; Moore & Esselman, 1992; Schunk, 1991; Tschannen-Moran & Woolfolk-Hoy, 2001; Tschannen-Moran et al., 1998), motivation (Midgley, Feldlaufer, & Eccles, 1989) and personal sense of academic efficacy (Anderson, Greene, & Loewen, 1988).

According to Tschannen-Moran and Woolfolk-Hoy (2001), efficacy also affects the effort that teachers "invest in teaching, the goals they set, and their level of aspiration" (p. 783). Teachers with a strong sense of efficacy tend to be more open to new ideas and more willing to experiment with new methods to meet the needs of their students (Berman et al., 1977; Guskey, 1988; Stein & Wang, 1988).

In contrast, teachers who have low self-efficacy "might avoid planning activities they believe exceed their capabilities, . . . expend little effort to find materials, and not reteach content in ways students might understand better" (Schunk, 1991, p. 224). Thus it is critical to look more closely at teachers' specific sense of efficacy (in this case related to teaching algebra) and ways of measuring in order to examine and support efficacy levels as they connect to student outcomes.

Several research studies in the area of self-efficacy have not produced the desired results with respect to its effects because of the lack of specificity of the self-efficacy measure (Pajares, 1996). This idea of the need for specificity is also noted in research related to self-concept theory, which is closely related to self-efficacy (O'Mara, March, Craven, & Debus, 2006). Self-efficacy beliefs are not always consistent among the various teacher responsibilities and subject areas (Bandura, 1997). This line of reasoning could be extended to imply that self-efficacy beliefs toward mathematics in general may be different than those concerning algebra specifically.

Additionally, according to Finney and Schraw (2003), self-efficacy is task-specific (e.g., simplifying an algebraic expression) rather than domain-specific (e.g., learning algebra). They argue that even though the domain-general self-efficacy is somewhat generalizable to specific tasks within that domain, "the closer the correspondence between the task and self-efficacy assessment, the better the prediction of performance on the task" (Finney & Schraw, 2003, p. 163). Tschannen-Moran and Woolfolk-Hoy (2001) acknowledge there are problems with some measures of teacher efficacy. Some issues relate to the question of context specificity and transferability across contexts as well as the appropriate level of specificity related to teacher efficacy.

There are instruments available to measure self-efficacy, teacher self-efficacy, and mathematics and science teacher efficacy of elementary preservice and inservice teachers but none specific to the content area of algebra. Similarly, there is a need for a more accurate measure of teacher self-efficacy that is content *and* concept specific with respect to algebra (Hillman, 1986; Usher & Pajares, 2008).

While McGee and Wang (2014) recently published an instrument related to measuring self-efficacy of teaching mathematics that did identify two aspects of self-efficacy, pedagogy in mathematics and teaching mathematics content, it covers multiple areas of elementary school mathematics. While it complements the work of this proposed framework, our work may extend their work and add a level of specificity and address secondary teachers that may be useful in measurement.

McCrory, Floden, Ferrini-Mundy, Reckase, and Senk (2012), developers of the Knowledge of Algebra for Teachers (KAT), reiterated this point when they wrote that "tools are needed that measure the types of mathematical knowledge thought to be useful for teaching" (p. 610). Subsequently they have developed an instrument to measure algebra knowledge using three types of knowledge: school knowledge, advanced knowledge, and teaching knowledge (Reckase et al., 2015). The key being that there are different types of knowledge needed, including knowledge of school algebra and algebra-for-teaching knowledge.

The literature review previously presented suggests a connection to efficacy. Thus it is critical to identify a sufficient level of mathematical specificity regarding a self-efficacy construct so that appropriate measures can be developed and then compared in line with what they measure. To do this a framework for measuring algebra teacher self-efficacy has been developed by the authors. What follows is a description of the process that was used to develop that framework.

METHODOLOGY FOR DEVELOPING THE FRAMEWORK

In an effort to identify the different aspects that defined the self-efficacy construct for teaching algebra, the research team conducted a thorough review of literature that informed the framework and then organized a data collection scheme that included a review and analysis of important documents that would yield the key elements for teaching and learning algebra. This qualitative research design was approached as a grounded theory study with the purpose of generating a framework for algebra teaching efficacy (Creswell, 2013). The theory was grounded in the data analyzed through the various standards and curricula documents that ultimately shaped the framework.

Initially one document was coded for key themes related to teaching and learning algebra; then another was selected and a constant comparative analysis was applied. This process continued until the framework was fully developed through identification of categories.

The team reviewed current efficacy instruments and conducted an analysis of curriculum and teaching standards related to algebra. A search was done to ascertain what efficacy instruments had been used in research. In particular instruments were selected using the following criteria: they were developed to measure some aspect of teacher efficacy, validated and reliability information was available, and they had been used by researchers.

Curriculum and teaching standards documents were selected using the following criteria: documents from government and national mathematics education organizations that expressly outlined or identified curricula organization and teaching standards for mathematics and select state mathematics curriculum documents (details regarding the state selection are provided later in this article). There were twelve efficacy instruments, six curriculum standards documents, and three teaching standards documents selected and reviewed. After selected documents were organized, the entire team worked together to review the current efficacy instruments and curriculum documents to identify key elements, structure and format, and content related to the teaching and learning of algebra.

It should be noted that the team consisted of ten university mathematics and mathematics education faculty from nine universities in south-central United States. The researchers were part of a group that had been attending the Mathematics Education Research in Texas (MERiT) conference organized by Sam Houston State University in Huntsville, Texas, for several years. One purpose of the conference was to bring state researchers together from smaller Texas universities and colleges to collaborate.

After attending for a few years, two of the authors made a presentation to the group to ascertain interest in pursuing research around mathematics teacher efficacy as there were several in the larger group who had that specific interest. Thus this team of researchers was formed and pursued research in algebra teacher efficacy. Almost all had previous K–12 experience ranging from two to eighteen years, with over half teaching at the secondary level in mathematics.

For the analysis of algebra curriculum and teaching standards, the team divided into two groups to examine the documents. One group focused primarily on teacher expectations, while the other group focused on learner expectations. The documents, which served as the primary source of data, were analyzed with a qualitative approach, as each group reviewed to determine emerging themes. As suggested by Huberman and Miles (2002), after the members of each group reviewed the selected material, they returned to the notes and attempted to identify the themes according to which the data could be further examined.

Each group had discussions to build agreement among the group and to organize the prominent themes. When the themes were organized, the information was shared between the two groups for verification of the data. These themes were further discussed with the full research team, practicing mathematics teachers and mathematics teacher educators. This work led to the development of a framework of algebra teacher efficacy.

Identification of Current Efficacy Instruments

Initially, the team identified current efficacy instruments related to teaching and learning in general and in specific content areas. These are listed and described in table 4.1. This was done in order to ascertain available instruments for measuring aspects of efficacy and thus providing a basis for the potential development of an algebra specific instrument by demonstrating a gap and a need.

Curriculum Analysis

The analysis of curriculum and teaching standards was conducted to determine the key concepts in algebra and pedagogical approaches related to the teaching and learning of algebra, resulting in the identification of behaviors related to self-efficacy in teaching algebra. This approach reinforces McCrory et al.'s (2012) suggestion that "test developers should begin from a framework, . . . laying out the major areas of mathematical knowledge for teaching algebra" (p. 610).

The researchers engaged in a two-stage process to organize and analyze the curriculum documents. First, matrices were used to organize the standards documents for students in algebra and for teaching algebra (Miles & Huberman, 1994). Second, the standards documents' expectations organized within the matrices were coded using a thematic analysis approach (Braun & Clarke, 2006).

First Stage

The research team was divided into two working groups; one analyzed the national and state standards for students in algebra and the second analyzed

Table 4.1. Description of Applicable Efficacy Instruments

Authors	Name of Instrument	Purpose
Riggs & Enochs, 1990	*Science Teaching Efficacy Belief Instrument Form B*	Two subscales: self-efficacy and outcome expectancy with respect to science teaching and learning; targeted audience: preservice elementary teachers.
Rubeck & Enochs, 1991	*Science Teaching Self-Efficacy Instrument—Chemistry (STEBI-CHEM)*	Measures self-efficacy in teaching chemistry; targeted audience: inservice teachers.
Enochs, Smith, & Huinker, 2000	*Mathematics Teaching Efficacy Beliefs Instrument (MTEBI)*	Two subscales: Personal Mathematics Teaching Efficacy (PMTE) and Mathematics Teaching Outcome Expectancy (MTOE); targeted audience: preservice elementary teachers.
Hoy & Woolfolk, 1993	*Teacher Efficacy Scale*	Two independent factors: Teaching Efficacy (TE) and Personal Efficacy (PE); targeted audience: inservice teachers.
Koul & Rubba, 1999	*Personal Internet Teaching Efficacy Beliefs Scale (PITEBS)*	Measures teachers' self-efficacy beliefs with respect to incorporating internet into instruction; targeted audience: inservice teachers.
Tschannen-Moran & Woolfolk-Hoy, 2001	*Teachers' Sense of Efficacy Scale (TSES)* (long form), *Teachers' Sense of Efficacy* (short Form)	Three correlated factors: Efficacy in Student Engagement, Efficacy in Instructional Practices, and Efficacy in Classroom Management; targeted audience: long form recommended for preservice teachers, short form, recommended for inservice teachers.
Harrell-Williams et al., 2014	*Self-Efficacy to Teach Statistics in Middle School Survey*	Measures levels of teacher efficacy specific to teaching statistics for PreK–12; targeted audience: inservice teachers.
Dellinger, Bobbett, Oliver, & Ellett, 2008	*Teachers' Efficacy Beliefs System—Self Form (TEBS-Self)*	Assess teachers' self-efficacy beliefs about tasks that are associated with correlates of effective teaching and learning, all within the context of their own classroom; target audience: inservice teachers.
Skaalvik & Skaalvik, 2007	*Norwegian Teacher Self-Efficacy Scale (NTSES)*	Measures teacher self-efficacy consisting of six subscales: Instruction, Adapting, Education to Individual Student Needs, Keeping Discipline, Cooperating With Colleagues and Parents, and Coping With Changes and Challenges; target audience: inservice teachers.
Siwatu, 2007	*Culturally Responsive Teaching Self-Efficacy Scale (CRTSE)*	Measures preservice teachers regarding confidence in their ability to engage in specific culturally responsive teaching practices; targeted audience: preservice teachers.
Siwatu, 2007	*Culturally Responsive Teaching Outcome Expectancy Scale (CRTOE)*	Assess teachers' beliefs that engaging in culturally responsive teaching practices will have positive classroom and student outcomes. Teachers had to rate the probability that a behavior will lead to a specific outcome by indicating probability of success; targeted audience: preservice teachers.
Pruski, Blanco, Riggs, Grimes, Fordtran, Barbola, Cornell, & Lichenstein, 2013	*Self-Efficacy Teaching and Knowledge Instrument for Science Teachers (SETAKIST-R)*	Measures approximate efficacy for science pedagogical content knowledge. Unifies perceived teaching ability and perceived grasp of content knowledge; targeted audience: K–12 inservice science teachers.

(continued)

Table 4.1. Continued

Authors	Name of Instrument	Purpose
Goddard, Hoy, & Woolfolk, 2000	Collective Teacher Efficacy Scale (CTE)	Measures collective efficacy. Reflects positive and negative dimensions of the teaching task analysis and personal teaching competence. First empirically developed collective teacher efficacy instrument. Developed on reasoned a priori theory; targeted audience: inservice teachers.
Block, Hutzler, Barak, & Klavina, 2013	Self-Efficacy Scale for Physical Education Teacher Education Majors toward Children with Disabilities (SE-PETE-D)	Measures preservice teachers' self-efficacy toward including students with disabilities in physical education classes. Contains three scales: intellectual disabilities, physical disabilities, or visual impairments; targeted audience: preservice physical education teachers.
Roberts & Henson, 2000	Self-Efficacy Teaching and Knowledge Instrument for Science Teachers (SETAKIST)	Measures approximate efficacy for science pedagogical content knowledge. Unifies perceived teaching ability and perceived grasp of content knowledge; targeted audience: inservice science teachers.
McGee & Wang, 2014	Self-Efficacy for Teaching Mathematics Instrument (SETMI)	Measures two dimensions: efficacy for pedagogy in mathematics and efficacy for teaching mathematics content; targeted audience: elementary inservice teachers.
Akbari & Tavassoli, 2014	ELT Teacher Efficacy Instrument (ELTEI)	Measures seven components: Classroom Management & Remedial Action, Classroom Assessment & Materials Selection, Skill & Proficiency Adjustment, Teaching & Correcting Language Components, Age Adjustment, Social Adaptation, and Core Efficacy; targeted audience: English language teachers.
Betz & Hackett, 1983	Mathematics Self-Efficacy Scale (MSES)	Targeted Audience: Undergraduates Measures three subscales: Mathematical Tasks, Mathematics Courses, Mathematics Problems that related to gender issues of anxiety and confidence.
Kranzler & Pajares, 1997	Mathematics Self-Efficacy Scale-Revised (MSES-R)	Targeted Audience: undergraduates Multidimensional measure of math self-efficacy. (See MSES in Table 1).
Taylor & Betz, 1983	Career Decision Self-Efficacy Scale (CDSE)	Target Audience: Ages 16 to adult Measures the five Career Choice Competencies of John O. Crites's Theory of Career Maturity: accurate self-appraisal; gathering occupational information; goal selection; making plans for the future; and problem solving.
Betz, Klein & Taylor, 1996	Career Decision Self-Efficacy Scale (CDSE) Short Form	Target Audience: Ages 16 to adult Measures the five Career Choice Competencies of John O. Crites's Theory of Career Maturity: Accurate self-appraisal; gathering occupational information; goal selection; making plans for the future; and problem solving.

the national and state standards for teaching algebra. The first working group examined algebra standards in four documents: National Council of Teachers of Mathematics (2000) *Principles and Standards for School Mathematics* (NCTM, PSSM), *Common Core State Standards-Mathematics* (CCSS-M) (NGA & CCSSO, 2010), *Texas College and Career Readiness Standards* (CCRS) (Texas Higher Education Coordinating Board & Texas Education Agency, 2008), and the *Texas Essential Knowledge and Skills* (TEKS) (Texas Education Agency, 2009; 2012).

The CCSS-M (grades 6–8 and 9–12), CCRS (grades 9–12), and TEKS (grades 6–8 and 9–12) were aligned to the NCTM *PSSM* standards (grades 6–8 and 9–12). Therefore, the NCTM *PSSM* expectations related to algebra were one of the dimensions of the matrix, and the expectations for the other three documents were aligned to each NCTM *PSSM* expectation. The NCTM *PSSM* standards were selected as the initial curriculum document for the alignment process because they were developed prior to the other standards documents and are broader in description of student expectations.

The second working group analyzed teacher standards by examining the *NCTM Standards for the National Council for Accreditation of Teacher Education* (NCATE) (NCATE, 2003, 2012), *Texas Examination of Educator Standards* (TExES) (Texas State Board for Educator Certification [SBEC], 2004), and the *Conference Board of the Mathematical Science Standards* [CBMS] (2001, 2012). In a process similar to that used for the student standards, NCTM Standards for NCATE (NCTM & NCATE 2003, 2012) and TExES standards were aligned to the CBMS.

The researchers began at a state level with Texas since it was the U.S. state that all the research teams were engaged within their respective institutions of higher learning, and it was one of the largest states not adopting the CCSS. To further strengthen the alignment the researchers also analyzed Virginia's mathematics curriculum document as another U.S. state that did not adopt the CCSS thus providing a representative sample of not only the CCSS but states not adopting the document as well.

In 2011, the Virginia Department of Education (2011) aligned their state mathematics standards with the *Common Core State Standards* (CCSS). A review of the Virginia alignment and CCSS documents indicates they were able to align all the Virginia algebra standards with the algebra standards from the CCSS. Descriptions of all the documents reviewed are found in table 4.2.

Further, the reliability of the alignment process was established in several ways. At least two researchers within each working group aligned the expectations for each standards document. These researchers identified and reconciled any differences in their alignments. Each working group then reviewed the other working group's alignment matrix and provided feedback.

Table 4.2. Standards Documents Reviewed

Document	Author(s)	Brief Description
Student Standards		
NCTM *Principles and Standards for School Mathematics* (PSSM)	National Council of Teachers of Mathematics 2000	Outlines the essential components of a high-quality school mathematics program and highlights references to research on what it is possible for students to learn about certain content areas, at certain levels, and under certain pedagogical conditions.
Common Core State Standards (CCSS)	The Common Core State Standards Initiative is a state-led effort coordinated by the National Governors Association Center for Best Practices (NGA Center) and the Council of Chief State School Officers (CCSSO) 2010	Defines the knowledge and skills students should have in K–12 education so that they will graduate high school prepared for entry-level, credit-bearing academic college courses and in workforce training programs.
Ready or not: Creating a high school diploma that counts.	American Diploma Project 2004	Identifies and describes benchmarks for mathematics to support student college and career readiness.
Texas College and Career Readiness Standards (CCRS)	Texas Higher Education Coordinating Board (THECB) and Texas Education Agency (TEA) 2008	Designed to represent a full range of knowledge and skills that students need to succeed in entry-level college courses and to be prepared for a wide range of majors and careers.
Texas Essential Knowledge and Skills (TEKS)	Texas Education Agency (TEA) 2009 and 2012	State-mandated curriculum guidelines that establish what every student, from elementary school through high school, should know and be able to do in each subject area.

Virginia Mathematics State Standards of Learning	Virginia Department of Education 2011	Minimum expectations for what students should know and be able to do at the end of each grade or course in mathematics; the 2011 document demonstrates how the 2009 Mathematics standards are aligned to the CCSS.
	Teacher Standards	
NCTM Standards for the National Council for Accreditation of Teacher Education (NCATE)	National Council of Teachers Mathematics (NCTM) and the National Council for Accreditation of Teacher Education (NCATE) 2003 and Council for the Accreditation of Educator Preparation (CAEP) 2012	Developed for teacher preparation, licensing, and advanced certification; describes the specialized content that teacher candidates should master; divided into sets based on the grade level candidates will be certified/licensed to teach.
Texas Educator Standards for Mathematics (8–12)	Texas State Board for Educator Certification (SBEC) 2004	Educator preparation standards focused upon the Texas Essential Knowledge and Skills (TEKS), the required statewide public school curriculum; reflects current research on the developmental stages and needs of children from Early Childhood through Grade 12.
Recommendations of the Conference Board of Mathematical Science (CBMS)	Conference Board of the Mathematical Sciences (CBMS) 2001 and 2012	Recommendations for the mathematical education of prospective teachers within mathematical sciences departments at U.S. two- and four-year colleges and universities.

The research team as a whole considered and addressed any discrepancies to finalize the two matrices.

Second Stage

The researchers coded the expectations in the two alignment matrices using thematic analysis. The process included identifying initial codes, synthesizing the codes into themes, evaluating the validity of the themes with respect to the data, and naming and defining the themes (Braun & Clarke, 2006). Initially, two members of the research team generated thirty-two codes that represented all of the algebra expectations in the aligned standards documents. Examples included the following:

- Recognize the difference between linear and nonlinear functions
- Use technology for teaching and learning algebra
- Represent relationships using tables, graphs, words, and symbolic rules
- Understand rates of change
- Differentiate between functions and relations
- Model and solve contextual and situational problems
- Analyze graphs
- Distinguish between explicit and recursive relationships
- Utilize concrete models (e.g., algebra tiles)
- Understand the role of variables
- Recognize differences between expressions and equations
- Make connections between symbolic expressions and graphical representations of functions
- Recognize and generate equivalent forms of algebraic expressions
- Solve quadratic equations using varied methods (i.e., using the quadratic formula, graphing, completing the square)
- Solve equations and inequalities using graphical and procedural methods (i.e., applying algebraic manipulations)
- Interpret representations of functions in two variables
- Judge appropriateness of symbolic representations
- Determine the type of function to model a relationship

The codes were organized into six categories (i.e., themes). To assess the validity of the themes in relation to the entire set of expectations represented in the matrices (Braun & Clarke, 2006), the researchers, other than the two who originally completed the coding, color-coded the expectations in the matrices with respect to each category. This process was based on the premise that if the six categories were a valid representation of algebra as presented in the standards documents, all expectations in the matrices would be color-coded.

At the conclusion of the process, virtually all expectations were color-coded with the exception of ideas related to pre-Algebra and Algebra II.

A discussion followed about the standards related to whether Algebra II content should be included or not. The consensus was to not include the standards related to Algebra II and to focus on Algebra I content given the focus on algebra for all. Generally that stance is related to the major concepts included in a typical Algebra I course. For example, logarithmic functions and trigonometric functions are not concepts that are typically covered in Algebra I. While these are algebraic in nature, they are higher-level concepts that are not part of the algebraic foundation targeted in this framework.

This effort provided the research team with common big ideas and themes covered in Algebra 1. A parallel framework could be developed for Algebra II, but for an initial step given the importance of Algebra I as a gateway course (see earlier arguments) the researchers focus on only Algebra I.

As a result of the systematic analysis of the documents and literature described in the previous section, the researchers conceptualized two main domains of efficacy: *efficacy to do school algebra* and *efficacy to teach school algebra* (see figure 4.1). These dimensions parallel recently defined dimensions by McCrory et al. (2012) and Roberts and Henson (2000).

McCrory et al. (2012) distinguish between knowledges of algebra for teaching, that is, *knowledge of school algebra* and *knowledge for teaching school algebra* respectively. Roberts and Henson's (2000) work identified

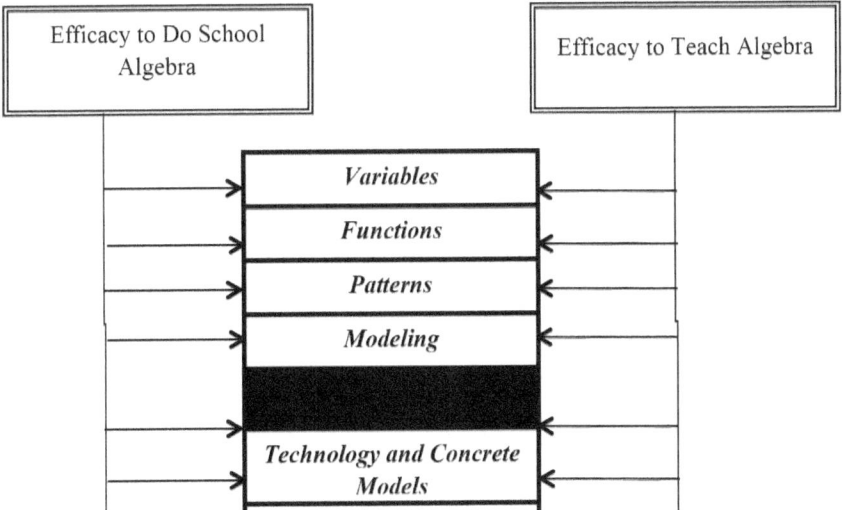

Figure 4.1. This figure shows the resulting framework for algebra teaching efficacy.
Created by Trena L. Wilkerson

two dimensions for science, knowledge and teaching self-efficacies, which are similar to the domains the researchers have identified for algebra. Further, McGee and Wang's (2014) self-efficacy instrument for teaching elementary mathematics also recognized two aspects of self-efficacy: pedagogy in mathematics and teaching mathematics content. Again, the idea of both content and teaching are reiterated.

In the framework presented herein, efficacy of school algebra refers to the ability "to do" the algebra taught in school mathematics. The ability "to do" school algebra we mean the ability to meet the expectations prescribed by student and teacher standards, which include the knowledge and skills of particular topics and processes. Efficacy of teaching school algebra refers to the ability "to teach" the algebra taught in school mathematics. By the ability "to teach" school algebra we mean the ability to teach others the algebra knowledge and skills expected to be learned in school mathematics.

But what is *school algebra*? As previously described, the topics and processes derived from the curriculum analysis were organized into six categories, four of the categories are content topics and two are processes. The four content categories are (1) variables (includes variables, expressions, equations, and inequalities); (2) functions (includes relations, functions, and families of functions); (3) patterns (includes patterns and sequences); and (4) modeling. The two process categories are: (5) technology and concrete models, and (6) multiple representations.

In order to clarify meaning, a description for each category was established. Building on the work of the NCTM *PSSM* (2000), the *Common Core State Standards* (NGA & CCSSO, 2010), and various state mathematics standards along with college and career readiness standards (see table 4.2), the following descriptions for each topic category were created:

- *Variables*: Understand the meaning of a variable as well as the different possible roles of variables; understand the difference between an expression and an equation; generate equivalent forms of algebraic expressions; solve and interpret the solution of linear and quadratic equations and inequalities; and analyze systems of linear equations in two variables using multiple strategies.
- *Functions*: Understand the difference between relations and functions; understand function notation; compare the characteristics of families of functions (linear and quadratic) such as rates of change, intercepts, zeroes, domain, range, and asymptotes.
- *Patterns*: Recognize and generalize patterns (e.g., arithmetic sequences and proportions).
- *Modeling*: Represent and analyze real world application problems.

- *Technology and Concrete Models*: Use technology such as dynamic geometry tools, graphing calculator technology, computer algebra systems, spreadsheets and concrete models such as algebra tiles and balance scales to explore algebraic concepts.
- *Multiple Representations*: Represent, select, apply, and translate between and among concrete models, tables, graph, words, and symbols.

CONCLUSIONS

Most efficacy conceptual frameworks are targeted at elementary levels and are not usually content specific. When they are content specific, they target elementary levels. We build on current research and new curriculum polices to develop a framework that it is specific to the efficacy to teach school algebra and that will aid in developing measures of this construct in the future. This teacher self-efficacy conceptual measurement framework is aligned with state and national standards in the United States for students and teachers as well as with some of the aspects of the conceptual framework of Knowledge of Algebra for Teaching (KAT) (McCrory et al., 2012).

At present, there are no teacher efficacy instruments that are specific to algebraic content or that specifically target secondary-school-level teachers. The development of an instrument targeting algebra teacher efficacy would add a valuable dimension to the study of efficacy among teachers and in particular teachers of mathematics. A more content and concept specific self-efficacy instrument would benefit both preservice and inservice teachers by adding a viable measure for both individual growth and program evaluation for teacher education programs and professional development initiatives.

It has the potential to provide information to teacher education certification programs as they prepare teachers and also to give professional development leaders important information as they work with mathematics teachers. If preservice and inservice teachers are assessed early, programs and interventions can be designed to assist in strengthening their algebraic content, content pedagogy, and beliefs about teaching algebra; thus impacting student understanding and achievement in mathematics which has implications for preparedness for college level mathematics and careers.

The measurement framework for efficacy to teach algebra includes knowledge of the content as well as instructional tools that support the teaching and learning of the subject. In addition, the framework includes the ability to use that knowledge to teach algebra effectively. These aspects are related to the conceptualization of pedagogical content knowledge (Shulman, 1986) and mathematical knowledge for teaching (Ball et al., 2008;

McCrory et al., 2012), which indicate that teachers need to know the subject area in ways that enable them to make that subject area accessible to the learners. Because of this relational and specificity level, the framework can be used to design tools to measure teacher self-efficacy as a gauge for the assessment of teacher knowledge.

Furthermore, the development of an instrument based on this framework has the potential to serve as a better evaluative tool for projects and programs related to teacher effectiveness when teaching algebra. Currently the research team is working on the development of such an instrument with a manuscript currently under review. New professional development initiatives as well as other initiatives to support teacher development require measuring their impact on student achievement in a particular content area. This framework and its potential uses offer a foundation to provide teacher educators, professional development programmers, school-level administrators, and mathematics leaders with a tool to measure and assess the impact of efforts related to student algebraic understanding that could be valuable in both the United States and other countries.

REFERENCES

Adelman, C. (2006). *The toolbox revisited: Paths to degree completion from high school to college*. Washington, DC: U.S. Department of Education.

Akbari, R., & Tavassoli, K. (2014). Developing an ELT context-specific teacher efficacy instrument. *A Journal of Language Teaching and Research, 45*(1), 27–50.

Allinder, R. M. (1994). The relationship between efficacy and the instructional practices of special education teachers and consultants. *Teacher Education and Special Education, 17*, 86–95. doi:10.1177/088840649401700203

American Diploma Project. (2004). *Ready or not: Creating a high school diploma that counts*. Washington, DC: Achieve, Inc. Retrieved May 29, 2014 from http://www.achieve.org/files/ReadyorNot.pdf

Anderson, R., Greene, M., & Loewen, P. (1988). Relationships among teachers' & students' thinking skills, sense of efficacy, and student achievement. *Alberta Journal of Educational Research, 34*(2), 148–165.

Armor, D., Conroy-Oseguera, P., Cox, M., King, N., McDonnell, L., Pascal, A., Pauly, E., & Zellman, G. (1976). *Analysis of the school preferred reading programs in selected Los Angeles minority schools*. Santa Monica, CA: RAND.

Ashton, P. (1984). Teacher efficacy: A motivational paradigm for effective teacher education. *Journal of Teacher Education, 35*(5), 28–31. doi:10.1177/002248718403500507.

Ashton, P. T., & Webb, R. B. (1986). *Making a difference: Teachers' sense of efficacy and student achievement*. New York, NY: Longman.

Ashton, P., Webb, R., & Doda, N. (1983). *A study of teachers' sense of efficacy* (Final report, Executive Summary). Washington, DC: National Institute of Education.

Bailey, T. (2009). Challenge and opportunity: Rethinking the role and function in developmental education in community College. *New Directions for Community Colleges, 145*, 11–30. doi:10.1002/cc.352

Balfanz, R., Legters, N., & Jordan, W. (2004). *Catching up: Impact of the talent development ninth grade instruction interventions in reading and mathematics in high-poverty high schools*. Baltimore, MD: Center for Research on Education of Students Placed at Risk (CRESPAR).

Ball, D. L., Thames, M. H., & Phelps, G. (2008). Content knowledge for teaching: What makes it special? *Journal of Teacher Education, 59*(5), 389–407. doi:10.1177/0022487108324554.

Bandura, A. (1977). Self-efficacy: Toward a unifying theory of behavioral change. *Psychological Review, 34*(2), 191–215. doi:10.1037/0033-295X.84.2.191.

———. (1997). *Self-efficacy: The exercise of control*. New York, NY: W. H. Freeman.

Berman, P., McLaughlin, M., Bass, G., Pauly, E., & Zellmann, G. (1977). *Federal programs supporting educational change. Vol. VII: Factors affecting implementation and continuation* (Report No. R-1589/7-HEW). Santa Monica, CA: The RAND Corporation (ERIC Document Reproduction Service No. 140 432).

Betz, N. E., & Hackett, G. (1983). The relationship of mathematics self-efficacy expectations to the selection of science-based college majors. *Journal of Vocational Behavior, 23*, 329–345.

Betz, N. E., Klein, K., & Taylor, K. (1996). Evaluation of a short form of the Career Decision Self-Efficacy Scale. *Journal of Career Assessment, 4*, 47–57.

Bishop, J. W., & Stump, S. L. (2000). Preparing to teach in the new millennium: Algebra through the eyes of pre-service elementary and middle school teachers. In *22nd Annual Conference of the North American Chapter of the International Group for the Psychology of Mathematics Education Proceedings*. Tucson, AZ: University of Arizona.

Braun, V., & Clarke, V. (2006). Using thematic analysis in psychology. *Qualitative Research in Psychology, 3*, 77–101.

Block, M. E., Hutzler, Y. S., Barak, S., & Klavina, A. (2013). Creation and validation of the self-efficacy instrument for physical education teacher education majors toward inclusion. *Adapted Physical Activity Quarterly, 29*, 184–205.

Brown, I. A., Davis, T. J., & Kulm, G. (2011). Pre-service teachers' knowledge for teaching algebra for equity in the middle grades: A preliminary report. *Journal of Negro Education, 80*(3), 266–283.

Chazan, D. (2008). The shifting landscape of school algebra in the United States: No Child Left Behind, high school graduation requirements, principles and standards, and technology. In C. Greenes & R. Rubenstein (Eds.), *Algebra and Algebraic Thinking in school mathematics* (pp. 19–33). 70th Yearbook of the National Council of Teachers of Mathematics. Reston, VA: NCTM.

College Board. (2000). *Equity 2000: A systematic education reform model*. Washington, DC: Author.

Conference Board of the Mathematical Sciences. (2001). *The mathematical education of teachers*. Providence, RI and Washington DC: American Mathematical Society and Mathematical Association of America.

———. (2012). *The mathematical education of teachers II*. Providence, RI and Washington DC: American Mathematical Society and Mathematical Association of America.

Creswell, J. W. (2013). *Qualitative Inquiry and Research Design: Choosing among Five Approaches*. Washington, DC: Sage Publications.

Davenport, E. C., Davison, M. L., Kuang, H, Ding, S., Kim, S., & Kwak, N. (1998). High school mathematics course-taking by gender and ethnicity. *American Educational Research Journal, 35*(3), 497–514. doi:10.3102/00028312035003497

Dellinger, A. B., Bobbett, J. J., Oliver, D. F., & Ellett, C. D. (2008). Measuring teachers' self-efficacy beliefs: Development and use of the TEBS-Self. *Teaching and Teacher Education, 24*(3), 71–766. doi:10.1016/j.tate.2007.02.010

Devlin, K. (2009). What is algebra anyway? *Education Blog*. Retrieved May 29, 2014 from Thirteen Celebration at http://thirteencelebration.org/blog/edblog/what-is-algebra-anyway/1081/

Enochs, L. G., Smith, P. L., & Huinker, D. (2000). Establishing factorial validity of the mathematics teaching efficacy beliefs instrument. *School Science and Mathematics, 100*(4), 194–202. doi:10.1111/j.1949-8594.2000.tb17256.x

Evans E. & Tribble, M. (1986). Perceived teaching problems self-efficacy, and commitment to teaching. *Journal of Educational Research, 80*(2), 81–85.

Finney, S. J., & Schraw, G. (2003). Self-efficacy beliefs in college statistics courses. *Contemporary Educational Psychology, 28*, 161–186. doi:10.1016/S0361-476X(02)00015-2

Gibson, S., & Dembo, M. (1984). Teacher Efficacy: A construct validation. *Journal of Educational Psychology, 76*(4), 569–582. doi:10.1037/0022-0663.76.4.569

Glickman, C. D., & Tamashiro, R. T. (1982). A comparison of first-year, fifth-year, and former teachers on efficacy, ego development, and problem solving. *Psychology in the Schools. 19*(4), 558–562. doi:10.1002/1520-6807(198210)19:4<558

Goddard, R. D., Hoy, W. K., & Woolfolk, A. (2000). Collective teacher efficacy: Its meaning, measure, and effect on student achievement. *American Education Research Journal, 37*(2), 479–507. doi:10.3102/00028312037002479

Goodlad, J. I. (1984). *A place called school*. New York, NY: McGraw-Hill.

Gorrell, J., & Capron, E. (1989). Cognitive modeling effects on preservice teachers with low and moderate success expectations. *Journal of Experimental Education, 57*, 231–244. doi: 10.1080/00220973.1989.10806508

Guskey, T. R. (1984). The influence of change in instructional effectiveness upon the affective characteristics of teachers. *American Educational Research Journal, 21*, 245–259. doi:10.3102/00028312021002245

———. (1988). Teacher efficacy, self-concept, and attitudes toward the implementation of instructional innovation. *Teaching and Teacher Education, 4*, 63–69. doi:10.1016/0742-051X(88)90025-X

Ham, S., & Walker, E. (1999). *Getting to the right algebra: The equity 2000 initiative in Milwaukee public schools*. New York, NY: Manpower Demonstration Research Corporation.

Harrell-Williams, L. M., Sorto, M. A., Pierce, R. L., Lesser, L. M., and Murphy, T. J. (2014), Validation of scores from a measure of teachers' self-efficacy to teach middle grades statistics. *Journal of Psychoeducational Assessment, 32*(1), 40–50.

———. (2014). Identifying statistical concepts associated with high and low levels of self-efficacy to teach statistics in middle grades. *Journal of Statistics Education, 23*(1), 1–20.

Henson, R. K. (2002). From adolescent angst to adulthood: Substantive Implications and measurement dilemmas in the development of teacher efficacy research. *Educational Psychologist, 37*(3), 137–150. doi:10.1207/S15326985EP3703_1

Hillman, S. (1986, April). *Measuring self-efficacy: Preliminary steps in the development of a multi-dimensional instrument.* Abstract of paper presented at the annual meeting of the American Educational Research Association, San Francisco, CA.

Huberman, A. M., & Miles, M. B. (2002). *The qualitative researcher's companion.* Thousand Oaks, CA: Sage Publications.

Hoy, W. K., & Woolfolk, A. E. (1993). Teachers' sense of efficacy and the organizational health of schools. *The Elementary School Journal, 93,* 356–372.

Ingersoll, R. M. (2004). *Why do high-poverty schools have difficulty staffing their classrooms with qualified teachers?* Report from Renewing Our Schools, Securing Our Future: A National task force on public education. Washington, DC: Center for American Progress and the Institute for America's Future.

Ingersoll, R. M., & Perda, D. (2010). Is the supply of mathematics and science teachers sufficient? *American Educational Research Journal, 47*(3), 563–594. doi:10.3102/0002831210370711

Kaput, J. J. (2000). *Transforming algebra from an engine of inequity to an engine of mathematical power by "algebraifying" the K–12 curriculum. Opinion Paper.* Retrieved May 29, 2014 from http://www.eric.ed.gov:80/PDFS/ED441664.pdf

Koul, R., & Rubba, P. (1999). An analysis of the reliability and validity of Personal Internet Teaching Efficacy Beliefs Scale, *Electronic Journal of Science Education, 4*(1).

Kranzler, J. H., & Pajares, F. (1997). An exploratory factor analysis of the Mathematics Self-Efficacy Scale-Revised. *Measurement and Evaluation in Counseling and Development, 29,* 215–228.

Leung, F. K. S., Park, K., Holton, D., & Clarke, D. (2014). *Algebra teaching around the world.* Boston, MA: Sense Publishers.

McCrory, R., Floden, R., Ferrini-Mundy, J., Reckase, M. D., & Senk, S. L. (2012). Knowledge of algebra for teaching: A framework of knowledge and practices. *Journal for Research in Mathematics Education, 43*(5), 584–615.

McGee, J. R., & Wang, C. (2014). Validity-supporting evidence of the self-efficacy for teaching mathematics instrument. *Journal of Psychoeducational Assessment. 32*(5), 390–403. doi:10.1177/0734282913516280

Midgley, C., Feldlaufer, H., & Eccles, J. (1989). Change in teacher efficacy and student self- and task-related beliefs in mathematics during the transition to junior high school. *Journal of Educational Psychology, 81,* 247–258. doi:10.1037/0022-0663.81.2.247

Miles, M. B., & Huberman, A. M. (1994). *An expanded sourcebook: Qualitative data analysis.* Thousand Oaks, CA: SAGE.

Moore, W., & Esselman, M. (April 1992). *Teacher efficacy, power, school climate, and achievement: A desegregating district's experience.* Paper presented at the annual meeting of the American Educational Research Association, San Francisco, CA.

Moses, R. P. (1995). Algebra, the new civil right. In C. B. Lacampagne, W. Blair, & J. Kaput (Eds.), *The algebra initiative colloquium* (vol. 2) (pp. 53–67). Washington, DC: U.S. Department of Education, Office of Educational Research and Development.

Moses, R., & Cobb, C. (2001). *Radical equations: Math literacy and civil rights.* Boston, MA: Beacon Press.

National Academy of Sciences, National Academy of Engineering, and Institute of Medicine. (2007). *Rising above the gathering storm: Energizing and employing America for a brighter economic future.* Washington, DC: The National Academies Press.

National Commission on Excellence in Education (NCEE). (1983). *A nation at risk: The importance of educational reform.* Retrieved May 29, 2014 from http://www.ed.gov/pubs/NatAtRisk/index.html

National Council of Teachers of Mathematics. (2000). *Principles and standards for school mathematics.* Reston, VA: Author.

National Council of Teachers of Mathematics Commission on Standards for School Mathematics. (1989). *Curriculum and evaluation standards for school mathematics.* Reston, VA: NCTM.

National Council of Teachers Mathematics and the National Council for Accreditation of Teacher Education (NCATE). (2003). *NCTM Standards for the National Council for Accreditation of Teacher Education* (NCATE). Reston, VA: NCTM.

National Council of Teachers Mathematics and the National Council for Accreditation of Teacher Education and Council for the Accreditation of Educator Preparation. (2012). *NCTM Standards for the National Council for Accreditation of Teacher Education.* Reston, VA: Authors.

National Governors Association for Best Practices and Council of Chief State School Officers. (2010). *Common core state standards for mathematics.* National Governors Association for Best Practices and Council of Chief State School Officers: Washington DC.

National Mathematics Advisory Panel. (2008). *Foundations for success: The final report of the National Mathematics Advisory Panel.* Washington, DC: U.S. Department of Education.

National Research Council. (1989). *Everybody Counts: A report to the nation on the future of mathematics education.* Washington, DC: The National Academies Press.

———. (2010). *Preparing teachers: Building evidence for sound policy.* Committee on the Study of Teacher Preparation Programs in the United States. Washington, DC: The National Academies Press.

———. (2011). *Successful K–12 STEM education: Identifying effective approaches in science, technology, engineering, and mathematics.* Committee on Highly Successful Science Programs for K–12 Science Education. Board on Science Education and Board on Testing and Assessment, Division of Behavioral and Social Sciences and Education. Washington, DC: The National Academies Press.

National Science Foundation. (2009). *Broadening participation in America's STEM workforce: 2007–2008 biennial report to congress.* Retrieved May 29, 2014 from http://www.nsf.gov/od/oia/activities/ceose/reports/2008CEOSE_BiennialReport.pdf

No Child Left Behind (NCLB) Act of 2001, Public Law 107-110, 107th Congress.

Norris, E. (2012). *Solving the maths problem: International perspectives on mathematics education.* London, England: The Royal Society for the encouragement of Arts, Manufacturers and Commerce (RSA).

O'Mara A. J., Marsh, H. W., Craven, R. G., & Debus, R. L. (2006). Do self-concept interventions make a difference? A synergistic blend of construct validation and meta-analysis. *Educational Psychologist, 41*(3), 181–206. doi:8081/1959.7/34252

Pajares, F. (1996). Self-efficacy beliefs in academic settings. *Review of Educational Research, 66*, 543–578. doi:10.3102/00346543066004543

Pruski, L. A., Blanco, S. L., Riggs, R. A., Grimes, K. K., Fordtran, C. W., Barbola, G. N., Cornell, J. E., & Lichenstein, M. J. (2013). Construct validation of the self-efficacy teaching and knowledge instrument for science teachers-revised (SETAKIST-R): Lessons learned. *Journal of Science Teacher Education, 24*, 1133–1156. doi:10.1007/s10972-013-9351-2

RAND Mathematics Study Panel. (2003). *Mathematical Proficiency for all students: Toward a strategic research and development program in mathematics education.* Santa Monica, CA: RAND.

Reckase, M. D., McCrory, R., Floden, R. E., Ferrini-Mundy, J., & Senk, S. L. (2015). A multidimensional assessment of teachers' knowledge of algebra for teaching: developing an instrument and supporting valid inferences. *Educational Assessment, 20*(4), 249–267. doi:10.1080/10627197.2015.1093927

Riggs, I., & Enochs, L. (1990). Towards the development of an elementary teacher's science teaching efficacy belief instrument. *Science Education, 74*, 625–637. doi:10.1002/sce.3730740605

Ringrose, L., & Adkison, J. (2009). Do students learn more with a certified teacher? A comparison of algebra students taught by certified and non-certified teachers. *Teacher Education and Practice, 22*(1), 10–28.

Roberts, J. K., & Henson R. K. (2000). Self-efficacy teaching and knowledge instrument for science teachers (SETAKIST): A proposal for a new efficacy instrument. Paper presented at the 28th Annual meeting of the Mid-South Educational Research Association, Bowling Green, KY (ERIC Document Reproduction Service NO. ED 448 208, Columbia University, NY).

Ross, K. (2014). Professional development for practicing mathematics teachers: A critical connection to English language learner students in mainstream USA classrooms. *Journal of Mathematics Teacher Education, 17*(1), 85–100. doi:10.1007/s10857-013-9250-7

Royal Society. (2011). *Preparing for the transfer from school and college science and mathematics education to UK STEM higher education.* London, England: Author.

Rubeck, M. L., & Enochs, L. G. (April, 1991). *A path analytical model of variables that influence science and chemistry teaching self-efficacy and outcome expectancy in middle school science teachers.* Paper presented at the annual meeting of the National Association for Research in Science Teaching, Fontana, WI.

Schmidt, S., & Bednarz, N. (1997). Raisonnements arithmétiques et algébriques dans un contexte de résolution de problèmes: Difficultés rencontrées par les futurs enseignants [Arithmetical and algebraic reasoning in a problem-solving context: Difficulties met by future teachers]. *Educational Studies in Mathematics, 32*, 127–155.

Schoenfeld, A. H. (2004). The math wars. *Educational Policy, 18*(1), 253–286. doi:10.1177/0895904803260042

Schunk, D. (1991). Self-efficacy and academic motivation. *Educational Psychologist, 26*(3–4), 207–231. doi:10.1080/00461520.1991.9653133

Shulman, L. S. (1986). Those who understand: Knowledge growth in teaching. *Educational Researcher, 15*(2), 4–14. doi:10.3102/0013189X015002004

Siwatu, K. O. (2007). Preservice teachers' culturally responsive teaching self-efficacy and outcome expectancy beliefs. *Teaching and Teacher Education, 23*(7), 1086–1101.

Skaalvik, E. M., & Skaalvik, S. (2007). Dimensions of teacher self-efficacy and relations with strain factors, perceived collective teacher efficacy, and teacher burnout. *Journal of Educational Psychology, 99*(3), 611–625. doi:10.1037/0022-0663.99.3.611

Stein, M. K., Kaufman, J. H., Sherman, M., & Hillen, A. F. (2011). Algebra: A challenge at the crossroads of policy and practice. *Review of Educational Research, 81*, 453. doi:10.3102/0034654311423025

Stein, M. K., & Wang, M. C. (1988). Teacher development and school improvement: The process of teacher change. *Teaching and Teacher Education, 4*, 171–187. doi:10.1016/0742-051X(88)90016-9

Stephens, A. (2008). What "counts" as algebra in the eyes of preservice elementary teachers? *Journal of Mathematical Behavior, 27*, 33–47. doi:10.1016/j.jmathb.2007.12.002

Taylor, K. M., & Betz, N. E. (1983). Applications of self-efficacy theory to the understanding and treatment of career indecision. *Journal of Vocational Behavior, 22*, 63–81.

Texas Education Agency. (2009). *Texas essential knowledge and skills*. Retrieved May 29, 2014 from http://ritter.tea.state.tx.us/rules/tac/chapter111/index.html

———. (2012). *Texas essential knowledge and skills*. Retrieved May 29, 2014 from http://ritter.tea.state.tx.us/rules/tac/chapter111/index.html

Texas Higher Education Coordinating Board, & Texas Education Agency. (2008). *Texas college and career readiness standards*. Austin, TX: Texas Higher Education Coordinating Board.

Texas State Board for Educator Certification (SBEC). (2004). *Educator standards for mathematics (8–12)*. Austin, TX: Texas Education Agency State Board for Educator Certification.

Tschannen-Moran, M., & Woolfolk-Hoy, A. (2001). Teacher efficacy: Capturing an elusive construct. *Teaching and Teacher Education, 17*, 783–805. doi:10.1016/S0742-051X(01)00036-1

Tschannen-Moran, M., Woolfolk-Hoy, A., & Hoy, W. K. (1998). Teacher efficacy: Its meaning and measure. *Review of Educational Research, 68*(2), 202–248. doi:10.3102/00346543068002202

Usher, E. L., & Pajares, F. (2008). Sources of self-efficacy in school: Critical review of the literature and future directions. *Review of Educational Research, 78*(4), 751–796. doi:10.3102/0034654308321456

Van Dooren, W., Verschaffel, L., & Onghena, P. (2002). The impact of preservice teachers' content knowledge on their evaluation of students' strategies for solving arithmetic and algebra word problems. *Journal for Research in Mathematics Education, 33*(5), 319–351. doi:10.2307/4149957

Virginia Department of Education. (2011). *Comparison of Virginia's 2009 mathematics standards of learning with the Common Core State Standards for Mathematics.* Retrieved February 5, 2015 from http://www.doe.virginia.gov/testing/common_core/index.shtml

Ward, E. K. (2009). *Latent transition analysis of pre-service teachers' efficacy in science and mathematics* (Unpublished doctoral dissertation). University of North Texas, Denton.

White, B. C. (2000). *Preservice teachers' beliefs: Nonrational to irrational to rational.* Paper presented at the annual meeting of the Mid-South Educational Research Association, Bowling Green, KY.

Wilkerson, T. L. (1996). *Teaching efficacy and teaching styles of secondary mathematics teachers.* Paper presented at the Annual Meeting of the American Education Research Association, New York, NY.

Williams, T., Haertel, E., & Kirst, M. W. (2011). *Improving middle grades math performance: A closer look at district and school policies and practices, course placements, and student outcomes in California.* Mountain View, CA: EdSource.

Woolfolk, A. E., & Hoy, W. K. (1990). Prospective teachers' sense of efficacy and beliefs about control. *Journal of Educational Psychology, 82,* 81–91. doi:10.137/0022-0663.82.1.81

Woolfolk-Hoy, A., Davis, H., & Pape, S. J. (2006). Teacher knowledge and beliefs. In P. A. Alexander, & P. Winne (Eds.), *Handbook of educational psychology*, 2nd ed. (pp. 715–738). Mahwah, NJ: Lawrence Erlbaum.

Chapter Five

Development of Chinese Teachers' Self-efficacy in a Professional Learning Community

Qing Gao and Jian Wang

The professional learning community features teachers working together in planning, observing, and critiquing their teaching (Cochran-Smith & Lytle, 1999; Fullan, 2007) and sharing ideas of curriculum and teaching practices (DuFour, 2004; Little, 2012). It is seen as a powerful mechanism that supports teachers in learning to teach effectively (Lewis, 2000; Louis & Kruse, 1995) and helps to improve their teaching practice (Fernandez & Cannon, 2005; Hiebert, Gallimore, & Stigler, 2002).

Teacher's self-efficacy is defined as teachers' confidence in their capacity to teach and to bring about student-valued learning outcomes (Tschannen-Moran & Hoy, 2007; Tschannen-Moran, Hoy, & Hoy, 1998). It influences teachers' motivation, passion, determination for teaching (Althauser, 2015; Hoy & Spero, 2005; Mergler & Tangen, 2010; Voelkel & Chrispeels, 2017), and supports teachers' decisions related to classroom management and instruction approaches (Tschannen-Moran et al., 1998), and thus, student performance-based systematic review of the relevant literature over the years (Zee & Koomen, 2016). Thus, it is reasonable to assume the professional learning community among teachers in school contexts can influence the quality of teachers' self-efficacy in teaching.

Chinese government has established and implemented the new curriculum and teaching reform in a top-down manner since 2011 that calls for teachers to help students develop knowledge and skills needed in the twenty-first century using school-based curriculum, innovative instruction, and rubric-based formative and summative assessment. Chinese teachers are organized to work with each other in several forms including the content-based group, grade level–based group, network learning community across different schools and informal learning groups (Qiao, Yu, & Zhang, 2018; Zhang & Pang, 2016), which to the extent resembles the professional learning community defined in the literature (Cochran-Smith; DuFour, 2004, & Lytle, 1999; Fullan, 2007). Therefore, it is reasonable to assume the ways in which Chinese teachers are organized to work with each other would shape their self-efficacy in teaching as expected by the curriculum and teaching reform.

This study examines this assumption by answering three related research questions: How do Chinese teachers perceive their activities in their professional learning community? Whether and to what extent does Chinese teacher professional learning community influence teachers' self-efficacy in teaching? What are the influences of other factors in the Chinese school contexts on their learning to teach in their professional learning community?

LITERATURE BASES

In this section the authors present an in-depth review of relevant literature for the study. Included is a discussion of theoretical frameworks and a review of empirical studies.

Theoretical Frameworks

Two theoretical frameworks frame this study. *The professional learning community theory* (DuFour, 2004) frames this study with two ideas. This first is the idea that the teachers' professional learning community influences teacher learning through the six related activities (Garet, Porter, Desimone, Birman, & Yoon, 2001). These activities include (1) different forms, such as workshops, group study, network learning, peer tutoring, and so on; (2) length, short-term or ongoing; (3) organization, for example, formally and informally organized; (4) focus, content, pedagogy, or assessment; (5) kinds, for example, plan, observe, or discuss teaching together; and (6) its coherence, such as consistent goals between individual and school. This idea serves as a conceptual base for us to judge the characteristics of the activities in Chinese teachers' professional learning communities.

The second idea is that the teachers' professional learning community is seen as useful in helping teachers develop collective understanding about the reformed curriculum standards, instructional pedagogies, and assessment strategies central to student learning and performances. This idea is used in this study to develop, verify, and interpret the central assumption that the existing forms of the Chinese teachers' professional learning community structured in their schools would, importantly, shape their understanding of the reformed curriculum, instructional strategies, and assessments, and thus increase their self-efficacy in teaching.

The *theory* about *the sources of self-efficacy development* also frames the focus of this study. According to the theory, one's self-efficacy in a specific area or field can be defined as "beliefs in one's capability to organize and execute a course of action required to produce given attainment of a task" (Bandura, 1977, p. 3). This self-efficacy is shaped importantly by four sources (Bandura, 1977; Tschannen-Moran & Hoy, 2001). They are (1) mastery experience, such as one's high performance in the relevant area and field; (2) vicarious experience, which is one's observation of others' effective approaches in a similar situation; (3) verbal persuasion, for example, the encouragement one receives; and (4) physiological states, such as whether one feels fatigue, aches, and pains resulting from his or her activities or experiences in the area or field.

This theory guides us to develop the coding system to identify the change of teachers' self-efficacy. It is also used to help us identify the important factors that shape Chinese teachers' self-efficacy in learning to teach under the reform contexts in addition to the traditional professional learning community structured in their school context.

Empirical Literature Review

To situate each of our research questions in the relevant empirical literature, we searched, identified, and reviewed the studies examining the relationship between the activities of the teachers' professional learning community, the development of their self-efficacy in teaching, and other sources that influence their self-efficacy, understanding, and competence in teaching as expected by the reform. This review led us to the following results.

First, several studies examined the relationship between the activities of professional learning communities and the change in teacher self-efficacy in teaching, which led to a conflicting result. Some studies identified a positive relationship. For example, Mintzes, Marcum, Messerschmidt-Yates, and Mark (2013) explored the effects of professional learning communities on science teachers' self-efficacy in teaching using control and experimental groups. It showed that participants in the experimental group demonstrated more significant and positive changes in self-efficacy in teaching than the control groups as they were involved in professional learning community activities.

A case study (Zonoubi, Rasekh, & Tavakoli, 2017) investigated the influence of two six-month professional learning communities on the self-efficacy of ten experienced teachers drawing on pre- and post-interviews, reflective journals, and recordings of the meeting of professional learning communities. It showed that the participants improved their self-efficacy when using innovative instructional and classroom management strategies. Another quantitative study (Porter, 2014) examined the relationship between professional learning communities and teacher self-efficacy, drawing on survey data with open-ended question items with teachers. It indicated that the professional learning communities were significantly related to teacher self-efficacy in both engaging student learning and classroom management.

However, other studies pose a question about the above results. For example, a study (Cowley & Meehan, 2001) examined the influences of a professional learning community on teachers' teaching self-efficacy in teaching reform-minded teaching with teachers in nineteen schools using two questionnaires. It found that teacher self-efficacy in teaching was not significantly associated with teacher's perceptions of a professional learning community in their school.

Drawing on the interview data with Chinese secondary chemistry teachers from two schools, Gao and Wang (2014) showed that while participants in one school felt that the Chinese teacher content-based group structured in their schools helped them understand the reform-minded chemistry teaching and increased their competence in teaching as expected by the reform; accordingly, those in the other failed to develop similar understanding and competence.

This body of empirical literature contributes to the understanding about the relationship between teachers' professional learning communities and teacher self-efficacy in teaching. However, such a finding has not been consistent in all the studies; especially, it is not established in the contexts of curriculum and teaching reform where teacher learning communities are officially structured in the schools. This study is designed to address the above limitation in the literature by examining the relationship between a teacher professional learning community in the context of reform in which a teacher professional learning community was officially structured in the school contexts.

Second, some studies examined the influences of several factors other than teachers' professional learning communities and how the nature of activities in teachers' professional learning communities may shape teacher learning. For example, in the interview part of the study by Mintzes et al. (2013), researchers found that the change in teachers' self-efficacy in teaching can be shaped any of the four sources, including mastery, vicarious experience, and emotional reinforcement in addition to teachers' professional learning communities. In a study that drew on survey data from 3,414 teachers and 186 principals in China, Liu and Hollinger (2018) revealed that the nature of activities in professional learning communities can be differentiated depending on the characteristics of the principal's leadership roles, which shaped teachers' self-efficacy in teaching differently.

Other studies examined the impacts of the culture of teaching in the school contexts on the activities of teachers' professional learning communities. For example, drawing on data of interviews and survey data with 175 Chinses teachers, Zhang and Pang (2016) examined the nature of professional learning community activities in seven Chinese schools and found that the cultural value of working harmoniously with others in learning to teach did not always exert the positive influences on professional learning communities in these schools. This finding is echoed in the study by Gao and Wang (2014) in that the teaching reform implemented through the centralized curriculum system and the content-based groups was always useful in supporting teachers in learning to teach as the reform expected.

Drawing on the survey data from teachers in thirty-one Chinese schools, Zhang and Sun (2018) found that the accountability system and the traditional collective and harmonious cultural values could shape the activities in teachers' professional communities differently by acting as a double-edged sword. That is, on the one hand, it promoted teachers' collective efforts in sharing teaching experiences and developing common teaching goals; while, on the other hand, it produced institutional and cultural barriers for teachers to learn to teach as expected by the reform.

This body of empirical literature suggests that the activities of teachers' professional learning communities can be swung by the different teaching cultures and curriculum assessment. However, the studies failed to examine how these factors influence the activities of teachers' professional learning communities and thus, teacher self-efficacy in teaching as expected by the teaching reform. This study is designed to address the above limitations in the literature.

METHODOLOGY

An exploratory qualitative case study is used to explore answers to the three research questions of this study. As Yin suggests (2017), such a case study is especially useful for the studies developed to construct an in-depth understanding of complex contextualized issues of K–12 schools in a social setting by uncovering multi-levels of data to develop a coherent set of conclusions. In this study, drawing on the interview and document data, we examined the complex relationships between the activities of teachers' professional learning communities in different schools, teachers' self-efficacy, and the factors shaping the relationships without any anticipated answers.

Participants and Contexts

Participants of this study were twelve Chinese teachers with six teachers from a K–9 school and six from a high school. These participants were purposefully selected based on two criteria: (1) they all participated in the activities of a teacher professional learning community during the study; (2) they reflected the range of teaching experiences, different genders, and content areas as shown in table 5.1 below.

The K–9 school was a public school established in 2016 and sponsored and managed by a nonprofit organization that generated resources for and managed a series of schools in different parts of China. As of April 2017, the school has thirty-three teachers recruited nationwide who are involved in three kinds of professional learning communities during the study.

First, all the teachers were the official members of the content-area group like those structured in most Chinese schools as described in the literature (Paine, Fang, & Wilson, 2003). In this group, teachers in the same content areas were grouped together to plan, observe, and discuss the issue of curriculum, teaching, and assessment relevant to the content as facilitated by the content-area group head and informed by the content-area leader in the district, who were working under the top-down the content-area groups pipe at city, provincial, and national levels.

Table 5.1. Biographic Information of Participants in Two Schools

School	Name*	Gender	Subject Areas	Education Level	Years of Teaching	Leadership Positions
K–9 school	Ma	Male	Mathematics	Master	2	
	Shan	Female	Mathematics	Bachelor	15	Grade-level head
	An	Female	Science	Bachelor	10	School staff head
	Yu	Female	Science	Master	1	
	Ou	Female	English	Master	13	
	Sherry	Female	English	Master	13	Grade-level head
High school	Yao	Male	Physics	Bachelor	32	
	Wei	Female	Physics	Doctorate	1	
	Liu	Female	Biology	Bachelor	23	Content-area head
	Yuan	Female	Biology	Bachelor	2	
	Chen	Female	Economics	Master	5	
	Wang	Female	Economics	Master	5	

*All the names here are pseudonyms.

Second, they were also the official members of the grade-level group. In the group, the homeroom teachers at the same grade level were grouped together to discuss the issues relevant to teaching organization and classroom management and planning. It also implements the grade and school level activities and events as facilitated by the grade-level group head, who also reported to school administration and those at the school district level.

Third, teachers were also grouped to receive professional training focusing on course design, teaching strategies, and assessments delivered online by university faculty and researchers and experienced teachers across different schools with curriculum and teaching expertise as facilitated by the nonprofit organization once a week. The training materials were accessible online. Training sessions were videotaped and teachers who missed a session could catch up by accessing them online. Once a year, teachers also had a chance to participate in a retreat where teachers from all the schools managed by the nonprofit organization got together for a week in one of the schools to exchange what they learned from the teaching and learning projects initiated and facilitated through the online training, such as the project-based learning project.

The high school was one of the top-performing public schools at the national level in the region with the K–9 school that has a seventy-year history. Teachers in the school were officially organized into four kinds of professional learning communities.

First, like those in the K–9 school, they were official members of the content-area group facilitated by the content-area group head. Second, they were also the members of the grade-level grades, who worked in a similar way as those in the K–9 school did. Third, with school support, teachers were required to build up the network learning groups with teachers from other schools to establish understanding of new developments and trends in teaching and curriculum relevant to their work in the school. Finally, some teachers also developed informal learning groups among themselves to share and try some teaching practices, such as project-based learning that they chose to implement in their classroom and such an informal learning group was not popular in the K–9 school.

It is obvious that the two schools had similar and different kinds and forms of professional learning communities institutionalized in each. These similar and different contexts and characteristics of the professional learning communities between the two schools allowed a chance for us examine the activities of teachers' professional learning communities and their functions as shaped by these similar and different characteristics.

Data Sources and Collection

This study used two kinds of data to generate the information and evidence necessary for us to answer each of the research questions in the study. First, three one-hour interviews were conducted with each of the participants: one at the end of October 2017, one in the middle of January 2018, and the other at the end of April 2018. The first interview establishes the participants' education background and teaching experience as well as the contexts in which they worked. The second allows participants to reconstruct the detail of their experience in different professional communities and their sense of self-efficacy in teaching in their school contexts. The third encourages the participants to reflect on the factors that influence their activities in the professional learning communities and their learning to teach.

The interview protocols for different interviews were developed based on the focuses of each interview as suggested (Yin, 2017). Following the suggestion by Seidman (2006), each interview was conducted with participants using the native language, Chinese, so that more accurate information could be collected. All the interviews were audio recorded. After the interviews, transcripts were completed using verbatim transcription (Creswell & Creswell, 2017) and then sent back for participants for checking.

Second, the document data, such as school curriculum, participants' unit plans, and so forth were collected. These documents showed how the reform policy was implemented and how teachers considered it in their teaching.

The above kinds of data were aligned with the information needed for answering each of the research questions in the study. Table 5.2 below shows such an alignment between each of the three data sources and information needed for each research question.

Data Analysis

We conducted the data analysis at two levels to develop answers to each of our research questions. First, we analyzed each type of data initially in the following ways. All the interviews were transcribed, coded, and grouped by themes related to the functions of participants' professional learning communities following the rubric developed and based on the theory of teachers' professional learning communities (Garet et al., 2001). Then, they were coded and grouped for the self-efficacy themes at the different points of time using the rubric developed and based on the theory of teacher self-efficacy (Bandura, 1977; Tschannen-Moran & Hoy, 2001).

In addition, these interviews were coded and classified for the themes related to factors influencing teachers' professional community as it emerged (Creswell & Creswell, 2017). The document data were coded and grouped the

Table 5.2. Alignment of Research Questions and Data

Data Source		What do teachers perceive their PLCs* work?				Whether and to what extent do PLCs change teachers' self-efficacy?				Whether and to what extent does Chinese culture shape PLCs?	
		Support	Collaborate	Content	Learning	Mastery	Vicarious	Encourage	Psychology	Collective	Harmonious
Interview	1	✓	✓	✓	✓	✓	✓	✓	✓	✓	✓
	2	✓	✓	✓	✓	✓	✓	✓	✓	✓	✓
	3	✓	✓	✓	✓	✓	✓	✓	✓	✓	✓
Documents	1					✓			✓		

*PLCs represents professional learning communities

themes related to the curriculum and teaching that teachers were expected to implement in their classrooms.

Second, we conducted analysis in the following ways to answer each of the research questions specifically. We integrated the relevant results from initial interview data analysis to develop answers to the first question, *How do Chinese teachers perceive their activities in professional learning community?* Then, we triangulated the relevant findings from the initial analysis of interview and document data to develop answers to the second research question, *Whether and to what extent do Chinese teacher professional learning community influence teachers' self-efficacy in teaching?* Finally, we synthesized the relevant findings from our initial analysis of interview and document data to generate the responses to the third questions, *What are the influences of other factors in the Chinese school contexts on their learning to teach in their professional learning community?*

FINDINGS

The authors report findings from the study based on their analysis of data. Included in the findings are three themes: community activities, improved self-efficacy, and context and culture impact.

Community Activities

Our analysis of interview data led to several findings about three kinds of professional learning community activities in each school's context. First, all the participants in both schools spent substantial time in their content-area groups in designing curriculum, instructional strategies, and assessments collaboratively central to teaching as expected by the teaching reform. As Ms. Wei, a physics teacher in the high school, claimed, "As part of the team, we created a semester-long solar cooking project and implemented it in the physics classroom. Now, I feel comfortable to use project-based learning." Consequently, the participants in both schools completed the development of the interdisciplinary course unit projects in three content areas, implemented these projects using project-based learning approaches, and then developed the rubrics necessary for continuously assessing students' progress in these projects as expected and facilitated by the content-group heads in the schools.

Second, the collaborative activities in professional learning communities in both schools shared the features of job-embedded professional development and were sustained with consistent focuses on curriculum, teaching, and assessment. For example, in both schools, the content-area groups had a specific scheduled time and place to meet weekly; this meeting was devoted to curriculum unit project development, design of relevant teaching strategies, and formative assessment rubrics as expected by the project-based learning ideas. As Ms. Chen, an economics teacher from the high school, said, "We have a fixed time slot and room for a weekly meeting. Because we stayed in the same office after teaching our lessons, it is convenient for us to share ideas."

Each group also coordinated time for its teachers to observe the implementation of these projects in the classrooms in and beyond their school contexts and to critique these lessons together. Many participants valued the opportunities that the content-area group created for them to observe and critique how their colleagues implemented the curriculum units and projects. As Ms. Shan, a mathematics teacher from the K–9 school, said, "Observing a public lesson in other schools helped develop our confidence in creating a school-based curriculum as we have more resources than other schools." In the interviews, Ms. Wei also valued the formal and informal discussions about lessons of experienced teachers in her content group activities that helped her develop "knowledge of teaching." As she said, "I took four times a week to observe Mr. Yao's lessons, which is a wonderful way to help me quickly gain knowledge and skills about teaching and learning."

Third, the regular weekly activities in the grade-level group and in the online learning communities in both schools played an important role in supporting the curriculum project development and implementation coordinated by the content-area group leaders with their unique focuses and approaches. In the weekly activities facilitated by the grade-level group heads in both schools, teachers worked together in identifying the issues and problems in teaching organization, classroom management, and individual students' behaviors that emerged from the implementation of the curriculum projects; they worked together to develop strategies and ideas to address them together as they occurred.

The online network learning communities in both schools became the places where teachers accessed the new curriculum module, instructional strategies, and assessment tools offered in the focused training workshops by the experts and the experienced teachers outside their school contexts. As Ms. An, a science teacher from the K–9 school, recognized, her communication with experts helped her understand the importance of learning theory and applying theory into practice. Ms. Liu, the head of the biology content group from the high school, also mentioned that the online networked collaboration created both opportunities and pressure for her colleagues while they were learning to teach as expected by the curriculum and teaching reform. In their interviews, all participants in the K–9 schools mentioned that they benefited from various activities created by the online community developed in their school.

Finally, informal group learning in the high school allowed teachers with different expertise and interests to collaborate with each other to pursue their shared interests, preferences, and needs in teaching and learning to teach. For instance, Mr. Yao, an experienced physics teacher, motivated five inexperienced physics teachers in the school to form an informal group to help inexperienced teachers improve their physics teaching strategies and class management skills by meeting together once a week. By joining in the informal experimental teaching group, Ms. Wang, an economics teacher, felt that she was able to have a chance to discuss and experiment with collaborative learning activities for teaching, which she personally found interesting but had no chance to learn in the other official groups. Such an informal group's activities, on the one hand, helped address the individual needs, interests, and preferences of teaching and learning. On the hand, it helped created a culture of teaching and learning which put the pressure on teachers to collaborate informally.

Improved Self-efficacy

Our analysis of interview and documents data also led us to several findings of increased teacher self-efficacy in various aspects of their work as expected by the curriculum and teaching reform shaped by their professional learning committee involvement. First, the development of local school curriculum was a more recent effort of curriculum reform in China to soften the rigid centralized curriculum system. Most participants claimed that they become more confident in developing the local school curriculum by infusing the active learning process in it through activities in the online network professional learning community in each school, in which they had chances to work with experts outside of their schools.

For example, ten out of twelve participants made such a claim in the interviews with them. As Ms. Wei, a physics teacher from the high school, said, "Through the professional learning community activities (online), teachers receive professional development and become more knowledg[able] about developing local school curriculum that they are not used to develop[ing]."

Second, moving teachers from more lecture-based teaching to a student-centered approach is another aspect of the curriculum and teaching reform implemented in both schools, initiated in a top-down approach in China recently. All the participants in the study felt more comfortable in moving from the lecture-based teaching to a more student-centered approach with five believing that they could conduct such teaching competently as a result of their involvement in the content-based group activities, including being mentored by experienced teachers in and outside schools and engaging in observing and discussing the public lessons by themselves and their colleagues.

For example, in the K–9 school, experts were invited from outside school to demonstrate how to analyze reform-oriented lessons for teachers in various content-based groups. Consequently, all the participants from the school maintained that such activities help them become confident in learning to teach accordingly.

Ms. Yuan, an inexperienced biology teacher from the high school who claimed the sixth-place award in a district-wide teaching competition, attributed her success in the competition to the support that she received in her content-based group. As she said, "I would credit the teaching award for the support that I received from my biology content-based group. My colleagues helped me polish my teaching practices through planning lesson[s] together with me, observing my teaching, and sharing ideas with me." Mr. Ma, an inexperienced mathematics teacher from the K–9 school, mentioned, "I only taught students in middle school for two years and never taught the 7th grade students before. By observing experienced teachers' public lessons, I have certainly improved in managing the grade-level students and becoming confident in teaching them."

Another area of curriculum and teaching reforms had teachers develop and use rubrics in conducting formative and summative assessments as a way to understand what and how students learn in the classroom, an assessment practice that teachers in both schools had not used to assess their students. All the participants in the study declared that they became more confident in using both formative and summative assessment based on the rubric that they learned to develop.

Participants perceived their confidence in doing so as shaped by the support that they received from the network learning community, where they could interact with experts and experienced teachers outside their schools who knew how to develop and use such a rubric. As Ms. Ou, an English teacher from the K–9 school, shared with us, "I never used rubric before, but now, I use it not only as a tool for examining student performance but also as a resource to guide students to learn."

All the participants, to the extent, claimed that their improved self-efficacy in developing curriculum, instructional strategies, and rubric-based assessments for teaching as expected by the curriculum and teaching reforms helped improve their student learning. For example, all the participants in both schools mentioned that their students became more interested and engaged in learning as expected by the reform and achieved better performances as they improved their teaching practice though their activities in the professional learning communities at the school. Ms. Sherry, an experienced English teacher in the K–9 school, commended the breakthrough-English camp organized by her English content based group: "This camp provided plenty of English activities, in which students felt interested and motivated."

Context and Culture Impact

Our analysis demonstrated that the centralized curriculum and assessment system and traditional cultural values could exert conflicting impacts on the activities of professional learning communities in both schools. First, teaching under the centralized curriculum and assessment system, teachers were required to teach by following the centralized textbook along with the national curriculum standards. They were also held accountable for their teaching and their student learning by the curriculum-based accountability assessment every year.

This context, on the one hand, allowed the schools and districts to arrange a time and select topics for teachers to collaborate on across different schools while at the same time created the pressure for them to implement the centralized reform initiated through the centralized curriculum and assessment system. For example, the leaders of the online networking communities in both schools agreed that such a curriculum and assessment system helped them decide the topics for the networking communities' training activities. They invited experienced teachers and experts for the activities, which was done without difficulty, as teachers were all required to implement similar curriculum and teaching reforms in their classroom.

Second, the traditional cultural values of respecting the experts' authority and working with each other harmoniously also made teachers willing to accept what was offered to them by the expert and experienced teachers in their group activities. As Ms. Chen, an economics teacher from the high school, said, "We respect authority and look forward to learning from them." Ms. Wang, an economics teacher from the same school, agreed: "We are required to use centralized textbooks, which is a symbol of respecting authority."

Third, however, teaching under such curriculum and assessment contexts with these cultural values could also prevent teachers within each group from developing alterative teaching practices and from critiquing each other's teaching, which challenges the official curriculum standards and authoritative teaching practices received from training from their group activities. Mr. Ma, a mathematics teacher from the K–9 school, argued that being respectful to the authority prevents teachers from developing innovative instruction skills. Ms. Shan also commented: "Too much emphasis on harmony may lead one to avoid conflicts with his or her colleagues, which may become a barrier to innovation."

DISCUSSION

The study has several limitations. First, only twelve participants from two schools were involved in the study and thus, the results of our analysis may not represent the whole picture of professional learning communities among teachers from different content areas and grade levels in the Chinese schools. Second, the two schools in the study are located in a region with high economic status in China, which were often able to attract better-educated and highly qualified teachers to work in these schools.

Hence, the findings from this study may not fit other areas in China. Therefore, more studies with larger sample sizes and different kinds of teachers from different grade levels in different contexts are needed to verify and extend the results from this study. Finally, we have not examined how teacher self-efficacy in teaching is translated into their teaching practices as observed and their student performances as measured instead of relying on teachers' self-report, which is an important issue calling for further research.

Nevertheless, this study doses contribute to the understanding about our research questions in several ways. First, this study indicates that teachers' professional communities embedded in teachers' workplace could influence their self-efficacy in various aspect of teaching as expected by the curriculum and teaching reform including developing local curriculum, student-centered teaching practices, and rubric-based assessments.

This finding is consistent with those findings from other studies using case analysis, experimental design, and survey instrument conducted in the western school contexts (Mintzes et al., 2013; Porter, 2014; Zonoubi et al., 2017). It also contributes to the empirical evidence for the assumed positive relationship between teacher professional learning communities and teachers' self-efficacy in teaching with a Chinese example, which is absent in the existing literature (Tschannen-Moran & Hoy, 2001). It further supports the theoretical assumption that one's vicarious experience, in which they have chances to observe others' effective approaches in a similar situation, is an important source for self-efficacy development with an example of learning to teach in the school contexts (Bandura, 1977).

However, such a finding about the improved teacher self-efficacy in teaching under the influence of teacher professional learning communities does not necessarily mean teachers with such an improved efficacy in teaching will automatically lead to effective teaching practices central to the quality of student learning as expected by the curriculum and teaching reform. Thus, future studies need to be developed to examine the relationship between teacher self-efficacy in teaching developed in the professional learning community, their actual teaching, and student learning exposed to such teaching as we mentioned earlier.

Second, this study suggests that the centralized curriculum system plus the traditional cultural value of respecting authority and working harmoniously with others could also nurture context support teacher learning in the activities of the different professional learning communities. In this context, teachers would respect the authoritative requirements of curriculum and teaching reform and work collaboratively to learn to implement such requirements in the activities of the different professional learning communities. This can especially be the case when such activities were developed to offer support for teachers to implement such reform.

This finding resonates with the findings of other studies conducted in China (Chen, 2006; Wong, 2010; Zhang & Pang, 2016) that showed the school-based teacher professional learning community was shaped, importantly, by traditional cultural values, such as harmony and respecting authority. It also indirectly supports the findings of empirical research over the years (Little, 1990, 2012) in the western context that the teacher professional communities are often hard to grow to support the external requirements of curriculum and teaching reforms when such curriculum and teaching requirements are authoritative and consistent with each other (Cohen & Ball, 1990; Cohen & Spillane, 1992). Even if such curriculum and teaching requirements are administratively institutionalized, teachers may not work appropriately as expected in the context if an individualist culture of teaching prevailed (Feiman-Nemser & Floden, 1986).

Third, this study demonstrates that working under the authoritative curriculum and assessment school contexts, and within the accepted norms of respecting authority and cultivating harmonious culture, teachers could be limited in their initiatives in two areas: (1) developing teaching strategies not consistent with the powerful curriculum and assessment system and (2) critiquing or challenging such policy implementation.

This finding echoes the observation about teacher professional communities in Chinese school contexts (Gao & Wang, 2014). It further supports the assumption that when teachers are organized to teach in the contrived collaboration among them, their creativity in developing innovative teaching practices and the competence to reasonably critique the external imposed curriculum and teaching reform can be curtailed (Cochran-Smith, 2001; Hargreaves & Dawe, 1990). However, such creativity and critique are central to the implementation of curriculum and teaching reform that has yet to be supported by the appropriate evidence or that is not tailored to the particular needs of students from different cultural backgrounds and from different regions (Gay, 2000; Ladson-Billings, 1995).

CONCLUSIONS

The study offers two implications for policy makers and program creators. First, the establishment of school-based teacher professional learning communities is necessary but not sufficient to ensure teachers' collaboration that will lead to the expected efficacy in teaching as expected by the reform. This can be the case even if multiple collaboration structures and time are created, since teachers learning to teach can be deeply rooted in the kinds of curriculum and assessment system, centralized or decentralized. Therefore, policy makers should consider the influences of the curriculum and assessment contexts under which teachers are learning and teaching when developing teacher professional learning communities in the school contexts to implement the reform (Cohen & Ball, 1990; Cohen & Spillane, 1992).

Second, in initiating school-based teacher professional learning community, sufficient consideration needs to be given to the cultural values that script teachers' teaching and learning-to-teach practices (Hiebert et al., 2002; Hiebert & Stigler, 2000). Because of the scripted nature of teaching and learning to teach, it is not reasonable to expect that the schoolteacher professional learning community will revolutionize teaching and learning to teach overnight. Sufficient patience and an infiltrative approach may be necessary.

REFERENCES

Althauser, K. (2015). Job-embedded professional development: Its impact on teacher self-efficacy and student performance. *Teacher Development, 19*(2), 210–225.

Bandura, A. (1977). Self-efficacy: Toward a unifying theory of behavioral change. *Psychological Review, 84*(2), 191–215.

Chen, G. (2006). A commentary on the teaching research group phenomenon in China. *Nantong University Journal, 22*(4), 1–4.

Cochran-Smith, M. (2001). Learning to teach against the (new) grain. *Journal of Teacher Education, 52*(1), 3–4.

Cochran-Smith, M., & Lytle, S. L. (1999). Relationships of knowledge and practice: Teacher learning in communities. *Review of Research in Education, 24*, 249–298.

Cohen, D. K., & Ball, D. L. (1990). Relations between policy and practice: A commentary. *Educational Evaluation and Policy Analysis, 12*, 331–338.

Cohen, D. K., & Spillane, J. P. (1992). Policy and practice: The relations between governance and instruction. *Review of Research in Education, 18*, 3–49.

Cowley, K. S., & Meehan, M. L. (2001, July 19–21). *Assessing teacher efficacy and professional learning community in 19 elementary and high schools*. Paper presented at the Tenth Annual Meeting of the CREATE. Wilmington, NC: National Evaluation Institute.

Creswell, J. W., & Creswell, J. D. (2017). *Research design: Qualitative, quantitative, and mixed methods approaches*: Thousand Oaks, CA: Sage.

Darling-Hammond, L. (2000). Teacher quality and student achievement: A review of state policy evidence. Educational Policy Analysis Archives, 8(1), 1–44. Retrieved from epaa.asu.edu/ojs/article/viewFile/392/515

DuFour, R. (2004). What is a "professional learning community"? *Educational Leadership, 61*(8), 6–11.

Feiman-Nemser, S., & Floden, R. (1986). The culture of teaching. In M. C. Wittrock (Ed.), *Handbook of Research on Teaching* (pp. 505–526). New York: Macmillan.

Fernandez, C., & Cannon, J. (2005). What Japanese and U.S. teachers think about when constructing mathematics lessons: A preliminary investigation. *The Elementary School Journal, 105*(5), 481–498.

Fullan, M. (2007). *The meaning of educational change* (2nd ed.). New York, NY: Teachers College Press.

Gao, S., & Wang, J. (2014). Teaching transformation under centralized curriculum and teacher learning community: Two Chinese chemistry teachers' experiences in developing inquiry-based instruction. *Teaching & Teacher Education, 44*, 1–11.

Garet, M. S., Porter, A. C., Desimone, L., Birman, B. F., & Yoon, K. S. (2001). What makes professional development effective? Results from a national sample of teachers. *American Educational Research Journal, 38*(4), 915–945.

Gay, G. (2000). *Culturally responsive teaching: Theory, research, and practice*. New York, NY: Teachers College Press.

Hargreaves, A., & Dawe, R. (1990). Paths of professional development: Contrived collegiality, collaborative culture, and the case of peer coaching. *Teaching and Teacher Education, 6*(3), 227–241.

Hiebert, J., Gallimore, R., & Stigler, J. W. (2002). A knowledge base for the teaching profession: What would it look like and how can we get one? *Educational Researcher, 31*(5), 3–15.

Hiebert, J., & Stigler, J. W. (2000). A proposal for improving classroom teaching: Lessons from the TIMSS video study. *Elementary School Journal, 101*(1), 3–20.

Hoy, A. W., & Spero, R. B. (2005). Changes in teacher efficacy during the early years of teaching: A comparison of four measures. *Teaching and Teacher Education, 21*(4), 343–356.

Ladson-Billings, G. (1995). Toward a theory of culturally relevant pedagogy. *American Educational Research Journal, 32*(3), 465–491.

Lewis, C. C. (2000). *Lesson study: The core of Japanese professional development*. Paper presented at the Annual Meeting of the American Educational Research Association, New Orleans, LA.

Little, J. W. (1990). The persistence of privacy: Autonomy and initiative in teachers' professional relationship. *Teachers College Record, 91*(4), 509–536.

Little, J. W. (2012). Professional community and professional development in the learning-centered school. *Teacher learning that matters* (pp. 42–64). London, England: Routledge.

Liu, S., & Hallinger, P. (2018). Principal instructional leadership, teacher self-efficacy, and teacher professional learning in China: Testing a mediated-effects model. *Educational Administration Quarterly, 54*(4), 501–528.

Louis, K. S., & Kruse, S. D. (1995). *Professionalism and community: Perspectives on reforming urban schools.* Thousand Oaks, CA: Sage.

Mergler, A. G., & Tangen, D. (2010). Using Microteaching to Enhance Teacher Efficacy in Pre-Service Teachers. *Teaching Education, 21*(2), 199–210.

Mintzes, J. J., Marcum, B., Messerschmidt-Yates, C., & Mark, A. (2013). Enhancing self-efficacy in elementary science teaching with professional learning communities. *Journal of Science Teacher Education, 24*(7), 1201–1218.

Paine, L., Fang, Y., & Wilson, S. (2003). Entering a culture of teaching: Teacher induction in Shanghai. In E. Britton, L. Paine, D. Pimm, & S. Raizen (Eds.), *Comprehensive teacher induction: Systems for early career learning*. Dordrecht, Netherlands: Kluwer Academic Publishers.

Porter, T. (2014). Professional learning communities and teacher self-efficacy (Unpublished doctoral dissertation). Newberg, OR: George Fox University.

Qiao, X., Yu, S., & Zhang, L. (2018). A review of research on professional learning communities in mainland China (2006–2015): Key findings and emerging themes. *Educational Management Administration & Leadership, 46*(5), 713–728.

Seidman, I. (2006). *Interviewing as qualitative research: A guide for researchers in education and the social sciences*: New York, NY: Teachers College Press.

Tschannen-Moran, M., & Hoy, A. W. (2001). Teacher efficacy: Capturing an elusive construct. *Teaching and Teacher Education, 17*(7), 783–805.

———. (2007). The differential antecedents of self-efficacy beliefs of novice and experienced teachers. *Teaching and Teacher Education, 23*(6), 944–956.

Tschannen-Moran, M., Hoy, A. W., & Hoy, W. K. (1998). Teacher Efficacy: Its Meaning and Measure. *Review of Educational Research, 68*(2), 202–248.

Voelkel Jr, R. H., & Chrispeels, J. H. (2017). Understanding the link between professional learning communities and teacher collective efficacy. *School Effectiveness and School Improvement, 28*(4), 505–526.

Wong, J. L. (2010). Searching for good practice in teaching: A comparison of two subject-based professional learning communities in a secondary school in Shanghai. *Compare, 40*(5), 623–639.

Yin, R. K. (2017). *Case study research and applications: Design and methods.* Thousand Oaks, CA: Sage.

Zee, M., & Koomen, H. M. (2016). Teacher self-efficacy and its effects on classroom processes, student academic adjustment, and teacher well-being: A synthesis of 40 years of research. *Review of Educational Research, 86*(4), 981–1015.

Zhang, J., & Pang, N. S.-K. (2016). Exploring the characteristics of professional learning communities in China: A mixed-method study. *The Asia-Pacific Education Researcher, 25*(1), 11–21.

Zhang, J., & Sun, Y. (2018). Development of a conceptual model for understanding professional learning communities in China: A mixed-method study. *Asia Pacific Education Review, 19*(4), 445–457.

Zonoubi, R., Rasekh, A. E., & Tavakoli, M. (2017). EFL teacher self-efficacy development in professional learning communities. *System, 66*, 1–12.

Chapter Six

The Role of Self-efficacy and Other Characteristics of Elementary Mathematics[1]

A Model to Predict Student Achievement

James A. Telese, Zhidong Zhang, and Maria E. Diaz

Teacher quality has been of importance for some time, especially in the age of accountability. Different aspects of teaching have been considered for measuring teacher quality, for instance, teaching skills and content knowledge. As Educational Testing Service (ETS) (2004) stated, "Greater emphasis should be placed observing and evaluating teaching skills and content knowledge" (p. 13). Without a doubt, a teacher should contribute to their students' achievement and enhance learning (Rice, 2003). Good teaching requires four types of knowledge that includes thorough content knowledge and knowledge of both generic and content specific pedagogy (ETS, 2004).

Studies have met with mixed results that statistically modeled contributions of teacher preparation and teacher experiences to student achievement (Greenwald, Hedges, & Laine, 1996; Hanushek, 1996). There have been studies that reported positive and significant results when more direct measures of teachers' general knowledge were used, such as verbal facility tests and mathematics basic skills (e.g., Harbison & Hanushek, 1992; Mullens, Murnane, & Willett, 1996). There are very few studies that have examined the relationship between teachers' knowledge and student achievement.

Harris and Sass (2007) examined the effects of various types of education and training on the ability of teachers to promote student achievement and found that more experienced teachers were more effective teaching elementary mathematics and reading. Darling-Hammond (2000) examined National Assessment of Educational Progress (NAEP) mathematics data and found a positive and statistically significant relationship among teachers' certification status, degree in the field, and student outcomes. Clearly, teachers' general intelligence, content-specific knowledge, or both, are factors that affect student achievement (Ball, Thames, & Phelps, 2008).

A study of the 2005 NAEP data indicated that middle-school teachers' mathematics college course taking was positively related to student achievement. Moreover, the students of middle-school teachers who reported receiving a small extent of professional development on how students learn mathematics, scored higher on the NAEP than those middle-school teachers' students who reported large amounts of professional development (Telese, 2012). These studies indicated that teachers' knowledge of mathematics and their knowledge of how students learn mathematics are important variables in fostering student achievement.

Although several studies have examined middle-school mathematics teachers' relationship with student achievement, fewer have looked at elementary teachers' characteristics other than content knowledge (Ma, 2010). The purpose of the current study was to examine the relationships among various elementary teachers' characteristics including background variables such as, self-efficacy, years of experience, courses in mathematics, pedagogical content knowledge, classroom activities, and student achievement.

RELATED LITERATURE

Drawing from the purpose statement, the authors conducted an in-depth review of related literature to provide theoretical framework for the study. The review included teacher knowledge, self-efficacy, classroom practices, and professional development.

Teacher Knowledge

It seems like common sense to have teachers who are knowledgeable in their field; yet, there is disagreement as to what kinds of knowledge are important that positively impact student achievement (Sadler, Sonnert, Coyle, Cook-Smith, & Miller, 2013). Beliefs about teacher knowledge shape policy related to teacher credentialing, teacher preparation, and professional development. Identifying critical knowledge for effective mathematics teaching has been a concern for some time (e.g., Ball, Lubienski, & Mewborn, 2001). Shulman (1986) introduced the concept of pedagogical content knowledge and believed it is an important facet of effective teaching.

Since then, there remains no shortage of ideas as to what constitutes good teaching. The American Council on Education (ACE) (1999) reported that a college degree in mathematics and having a mathematics teaching certification contributed to an effective teaching of mathematics. This subject matter knowledge is defined as the general conceptual understanding of a subject area possessed by a teacher (Shulman, 1986). Most teacher preparation programs would agree that an understanding of content matters for teaching (Ball, Thames, & Phelps, 2008). When mathematics teachers' content knowledge is used as a variable in research studies, teachers' subject matter knowledge is often operationally defined as college major, courses, and types of courses taken (Wilson, Floden, & Ferini-Mundy, 2002).

Furthermore, it is assumed that student achievement often parallels student success (Tchoshanov, Lesser, & Salazar, 2008). Harris and Sass (2007) examined various types of education and training on the ability of teachers to improve student achievement using estimate models that include detailed measures of preservice and inservice training, a rich set of time-varying covariates, and student, teacher, and school fixed effects. Their results indicated that the more experience an elementary teacher had, the more effective the teacher was at teaching mathematics. In addition, the scholastic aptitude of teachers does not influence their ability to improve student achievement.

Yet questions still remain unanswered, such as what knowledge do teachers have and what is the nature of that knowledge? According to Ball et al. (2001), each of these questions should be answered. Direct measures of teachers' knowledge have been developed, based on Shulman's early work (1996), by Ball et al. (2001). These researchers found evidence that teaching mathematics required specialized content knowledge that went beyond a "pure" subject matter knowledge to one integrated with knowledge of students.

A study by Sadler, Sonnert, Coyle, Cook-Smith, and Miller (2013) attempted to measure science pedagogical content knowledge and its relationship to student achievement. These authors found that students with high mathematics and reading scores and whose teachers had high subject-matter knowledge, and awareness of student misconceptions, made significant gains in science understanding.

Moreover, Tchoshanov (2011) established three categories of teacher knowledge: (a) knowledge of facts and procedures, requiring memorization of facts, definitions, formulas, properties and rules, using procedures and solving routine problems; (b) knowledge of concepts and connections, which includes understanding concepts, making connections, using multiple representations and solving non-routine problems; and (c) knowledge of models and generalizations described as the teachers' knowledge and thinking for mathematics processes of modeling, conjecturing, and proving theorems. Tchoshanov (2011) conducted a correlational study between type of middle-school mathematics teachers' knowledge and student achievement and found that the second category, "knowledge of concepts and connections," was positively associated with student achievement.

Other factors can affect student achievement such as teaching experience as measured by the average number of years in service. Fetler (2001) found that teaching experience was positively related to students' test results. However, in a multiple regression study conducted by Kane, Taylor, Tyler, and Wooten (2011), teaching experience was found to have had marginal effect on student achievement. Also, schools with well-prepared teachers tend to have higher mathematics scores, whether preparation is measured as percent of mathematics teachers with emergency permits or as an education level index. This suggests that schools with experienced teachers who were well prepared tend to have greater achievement (Fetler, 2001).

Self-efficacy

The importance of a sense of self as a mathematics teacher was identified in the National Council of Teachers of Mathematics (NCTM) *Professional Standards for Teaching Mathematics* (1991) publication. It is noted that a sense of self takes time and develops over varied experiences in teaching and that one's self as a teacher is reinforced by feedback from students. This view develops and becomes stronger as their students appear to be learning mathematics. Thus, through interactions with students, it is recognized that they learn as a result of how the teacher shows confidence and exhibits flexibility and comfort with mathematical knowledge in his/her teaching (NCTM, 1991).

In a study conducted by Drake, Spillane, & Hufferd-Ackles (2001), elementary teachers reported to have low self-esteem about mathematics teaching related very positive life experiences in reading and felt more confident in teaching reading. For many elementary teachers this sense of self as a confident teacher of mathematics is difficult to obtain due to a high level of mathematics anxiety (Sowder, 2007). Perhaps, the source of this anxiety flows from a lack of understanding of mathematics, negative experiences with mathematics from a young age, or from their own teachers who also had mathematics anxiety.

Self-efficacy is viewed as one's belief in his or her capabilities toward mathematics and mathematics teaching. Teachers' personal self-efficacy consists of beliefs that contribute to the academic success of their students and influences how to teach mathematics (Midgley et al., 2000). Personal self-efficacy for teaching mathematics is a powerful belief (Throndsen & Turmo, 2013). Yet, there is a common social acceptance that having math phobia is "no big deal." This phobia tends to filter down to the elementary teachers and would be exhibited as low self-efficacy in mathematics or mathematics teaching (Kahle, 2008). As noted above, elementary teachers may have poor self-efficacy due to a lack of mathematics background knowledge and bad experiences when learning mathematics themselves.

Moreover, teacher self-efficacy tends to influence their choice of activity, levels of effort, persistence in students, and student achievement (Schunk & Pajares, 2009). Self-efficacy for teaching is a future-oriented, task-specific judgment (Throndsen & Turmo, 2013). Teachers with strong self-efficacy can have positive consequences for students (Butler & Shibaz, 2008). In addition, teachers with high levels of efficacy are inclined to develop challenging activities, help students succeed, and persist with students having problems (Schunk, Pintrich, & Meece, 2008). Hence, what teachers think of themselves as mathematics teachers impacts the teaching goals they set for themselves, the effort invested in reaching those goals, and their persistence when facing difficulties (Throndsen & Turmo, 2013).

Related to self-efficacy, is the goal orientation theory (Schunk et al., 2008). This theory represents a social-cognitive approach to motivation, and the goal orientation theorists argue that students' personal goal orientation is influenced by their teacher's instructional practices in the classroom (Schunk et al. 2008). Research on elementary teachers' goal orientations and instructional practices is limited (Throndsen & Turmo, 2013). A positive relationship was found between personal self-efficacy and student achievement, and performance in mathematics with teachers' goal orientations and practices (Throndsen & Turmo, 2013). Thus, it becomes important to consider instructional practices that possibly influence student achievement (Meece, Anderman, & Anderman, 2006).

Classroom Practices

The NCTM (2000) has long advocated the use of standards-base, student-centered learning approaches in which students construct their knowledge through engagement with complex tasks. This type of mathematics teaching includes the use of communication/dialogue in the classroom, the use of representations, making connections, making conjectures, and analyzing various approaches to problem solving. Thompson (2009) identified, through a multiple-regression analysis, three standards-based instructional strategies that were positively associated with student achievement: (a) use of hands-on materials, (b) self-assessments, and (c) project-based activities.

Similarly, Kane et al (2011) examined the relationship between mathematics teachers' evaluation of classroom practices and student achievement by using formal teacher observations. They found that overall instructional practices were positively related to student achievement; in particular, of the overall instructional practices, discourse and questioning strategies, where the teacher engages students in discourse and uses thought-provoking questions to explore and extend content knowledge, were positively associated with student achievement. Pressing for understanding is an important aspect of quality mathematics pedagogical practice (Kazemi & Franke, 2004).

The use of various representations is a critical element in developing mathematics concepts (NCTM, 2000). Pape, Bell, and Yetkin (2003) found that a feature in classroom instruction that emerged, as an essential component to seventh-grade students' learning of mathematics, was the use of multiple representations. The authors found that, multiple representations eased their cognitive load by providing conceptual tools for thinking when students were engaged in solving rich problems and accomplished significant mathematical thinking. With these conceptual tools, students were then better poised to explain an answer or solution method to a rich task, as well as to examine similarities and differences among solutions that promote conceptual understanding (Anthony & Walshaw, 2009; Suh & Seshaiyer, 2017).

Students' ideas become resources for learning from one another; their representations stimulate others' thinking, and their explanations challenge and extend the development of mathematical understanding (Bass & Ball, 2003). However, it is the role of the teacher to orchestrate this discourse, "one who can hear the mathematics in students' talk, who can shape and offer problems of an adequate size and sufficient scope, and who can steer such problems to a productive point" (Bass & Ball, 2003, p. vii).

Hence, aspects of instructional practices that develop elementary students' mathematical thinking include promoting collaborative problem solving, using challenging questions for follow-up, generating and evaluating alternative solutions to problems, and highlighting and discussing errors (NCTM, 2014). Consequently, teachers' instructional practices in turn influence students' goal orientations, which is a function of instruction, tasks, and activities that take place in the classroom (Throndsen & Turmo, 2013). In order to continue to be effective teachers, elementary mathematics teachers should seek professional development opportunities.

Professional Development

Life-long learning has been long associated with teacher professional development. Professional development is often viewed as being fragmented and on an as-needed basis, and relatively superficial (Loucks-Horsley, Love, Stiles, Mundry, & Hewson, 2003). Professional development activities that may improve teachers' knowledge and skills range from formal, structured topic-specific workshops to informal discussions in hallways (Desimone, 2009). There is a trend in teachers' professional development to connect it to student learning with an ultimate goal of closing achievement gaps among student groups (Desimone, 2009; Loucks-Horsley et al., 2003). A framework visualized by Desimone (2009) was used to study the effects of professional development, which included context for which it occurs.

The context included teacher characteristics, such as experience, knowledge, beliefs, and attitudes (e.g., Franke, Carpenter, Levi, & Fennema, 2001), and student characteristics, such as achievement and socioeconomic status (Darling-Hammond & Sykes, 1999). In Desimone's model, context had the potential to influence the core components of professional development and its outcomes related to the teachers and students. A study of professional development core features with middle and elementary school teachers was conducted by Copur-Gencturk, Plowman, and Bai (2019); they found that a focus on curricular content knowledge and examining student work were positively related to teachers' learning.

There have been few studies that have examined the context of professional development on student achievement. Penuel, Fishman, Yamaguchi, and Gallagher (2007) examined the implementation of the GLOBE earth science program by surveying their teachers about their knowledge, and how they changed and continued with professional development. Telese (2012) used a national database to determine the relationship among context variables and student achievement. The current study directly examined the relationship among elementary teachers' contextual factors such as self-efficacy, pedagogical content knowledge, professional development, classroom strategies, and student achievement.

METHODOLOGY

This study examined the relationship among elementary mathematics teachers' characteristics such as self-efficacy, pedagogical content knowledge, years of teaching experience, amount of coursework in mathematics, classroom activities, and student achievement. A path analysis was conducted using AMOS software. In this section the authors discuss the participants and the instruments used for data collection.

Participants

There were forty-five elementary teachers who volunteered to participate in the study. There were 171 students from this subset of teachers. The school district is located in Deep South Texas and is considered a poor district, with a large proportion of students coming from low socioeconomic conditions. In 2017, the U.S. Census Bureau (2019) reported that the per capita income was $13,292 with 37 percent of the population living in poverty.

Instruments

The authors used two instruments to collect data. The first instrument was designed to measure teacher background characteristics and the second instrument was designed to measure self-efficacy.

Teacher Background Characteristics

Number Concepts was measured using the Learning Mathematics for Teaching (LMT) instrument, which was developed at the University of Michigan. The reliability of the instrument was determined to be 0.83. The LMT-Number Concepts was selected since most of the work of teaching mathematics at the elementary level involves the learning of number concepts. The instrument includes a survey to gather background teacher characteristics: years of experience, number of courses taken in mathematics, other courses in mathematics education, and classroom practices.

There were six classroom items on the survey. This section asked teachers to respond to the question "How often do students in your mathematics class do the following?" A Likert scale was used ranging from 1 (never) to 6 (everyday), where 2 was "less than once a month," 3 indicated "1 to 3 times per month," 4 indicated "1 to 2 times per week," and 5 indicated "3 to 4 times per week."

Self-efficacy

Self-efficacy was measured using a twenty-one-item survey adapted from Enoch, Smith, and Huinker (2000). The survey was adapted for use with inservice teachers. Statements with a future tense were modified to present tense. The survey has two sub-scales, Personal Mathematics Teaching Efficacy Belief (PE) and Outcomes Expectancy (OE). Teachers responded to a Likert-type scale where 1 indicated "strongly disagree," 2 indicated "disagree," 3 indicated "uncertainty," 4 indicated "agree" and 5 "strongly agree." Items for PE were statements such as "I continually find better ways to teach mathematics" and "Even if I try very hard, I seem not to teach mathematics as well as I should."

Items for OE were statements such as "When a student does better than usual in mathematics, it is often because the teacher exerted extra effort" and "When the mathematics grades of student improves, it is often due to their teacher having found a more effective teaching approach." There are eight OE statements and thirteen PE statements on the survey. The criterion variable was the teachers' student mathematics scale scores on the state's accountability measure, which were used as the criterion variable. A path analysis was conducted using AMOS software.

RESULTS

A path analysis was conducted using AMOS software. The theoretical model produced a GFI of 0.753. However, the model indicated that the influence of pedagogical content knowledge and self-efficacy in combination with the other variables was not as strong as expected on students' mathematics achievement. The model showed that years of teaching experience and self-efficacy had a greater influence on student achievement. In this section the results are discussed.

Correlational Analysis

The Pearson Correlation Coefficients are presented for the background variables. There was a negative relationship between Years Teaching and both Course Work for Methods of Teaching Mathematics and Course Work in Math, $r = -.45$, $p < 0.001$ and -0.20, $p = 0.01$ respectively. This suggests that the longer an elementary teacher has taught, the fewer courses in both content and content pedagogy are taken. Also, there was a positive relationship between Years Teaching and Personal Self-efficacy for Teaching Math (PSE) and the Total Self-efficacy score, $r = 0.90$ and $r = 0.62$, $p < 0.001$ respectively. This result suggests that the longer an elementary teacher has taught the more confident they are in teaching mathematics (see table 6.1).

Yet, there was no relationship between Years Teaching and Achievement. A surprising negative relationship was indicated for Course Work in Math Methods and Outcome Expectations (OE) with an $r = -0.81$, $p < 0.001$ and Achievement, $r = 0.229$, $p = 0.03$. This indicated that the more course work in how to teach math, the less confident teachers are of their outcomes and there was lower achievement. Yet, there was a positive relationship with Total Self-efficacy $r = 0.172$, $p < 0.025$, suggesting that elementary teachers become confident when they have more courses in how to teach mathematics.

Table 6.1. Correlations among Professional Experience in Math, Course Work in Math, Self-Efficacy, and Mathematics Achievement

	Professional Experience in Math	Course Work in Math	Personal Self-efficacy	Outcomes Expectancy	Total Self-efficacy	Scale Score
Professional Experience in Math	1	–.085	–.114	–.812**	.172*	–.229**
Course Work in Math	–.085	1	–.510**	–.054	–.766**	.302**
Personal Self-efficacy	–.114	–.510**	1	–.243**	.882**	–.130
Outcomes Expectancy	–.812**	–.054	–.243**	1	–.355**	.158*
Total Self-efficacy	.172*	–.766**	.882**	–.355**	1	–.261**
Scale Score	–.229**	.302**	–.130	.158*	–.261**	1

*Correlation is significant at the 0.05 level (2-tailed).
**Correlation is significant at the 0.01 level (2-tailed).

However, a similar negative relationship was indicated for Course Work in Math and PSE, $r = -0.51$ and $r = -0.77$, respectively with $p < 0.001$. Course Work in Math was positively related to Student Achievement, $r = 0.30$, $p < 0.001$. This finding is consistent with the notion that mathematics content knowledge is helpful in teaching elementary mathematics (Ma, 2010). Elementary teachers' OE self-efficacy was positively associated with Student Achievement, $r = 0.158$, $p = 0.039$. This suggests that when elementary teachers feel that their student outcomes are related to what the teacher does then there is higher achievement.

An incongruent finding is that a negative relationship was found between Student Achievement and the Total Self-efficacy score, which included both Outcomes Expectations and Personal Self-efficacy for Teaching Mathematics

Table 6.2. Correlations between Years Teaching, Professional Experience in Math, Self-Efficacy, and Course Work in Math

	Years Teaching	Professional Experience in Math	Personal Self-efficacy	Total Self-efficacy	Course Work in Math
Years Teaching	1	–.447**	.901**	.622**	–.197**
Professional Experience in Math	–.447**	1	–.114	.172*	–.085
Personal Self-efficacy	.901**	–.114	1	.882**	–.510**
Total Self-efficacy	.622**	.172*	.882**	1	–.766**
Course Work in Math	–.197**	–.085	–.510**	–.766**	1

*Correlation is significant at the 0.05 level (2-tailed).
**Correlation is significant at the 0.01 level (2-tailed).

$r = -0.26$, $p < 0.01$. This finding indicated that when an elementary teacher's self-efficacy is low, then there is higher student achievement; low confidence translates into higher achievement (see table 6.2).

Composite Causal Modeling

Several causal relationship models were developed to examine the relationships of these background variables, including professional experience in math, course work in math, self-efficacy, outcomes expectations, and students' achievement. The purpose was to examine several alternative models in order to highlight some specific relations in these models.

The Path Model Focusing on Student Achievement

In this model, we include Years Teaching, Course Work in Math, Course Work in Math Methods, and student achievement. The research question can be posed as "How does teaching experience influence student achievement mediated by Course Work in both mathematics and math methods?"

In this model, the GFI = 0.967, which indicates that the model fits very well. Figure 6.1 illustrates that there is a negative association between Years Teaching (YWE) and Course Work in Math. Also, there is a negative association between Years Teaching (YWE) and Course Work in Math Methods. However, these three variables all show a positive association with student achievement (Scale Score). Years of Teaching Experience

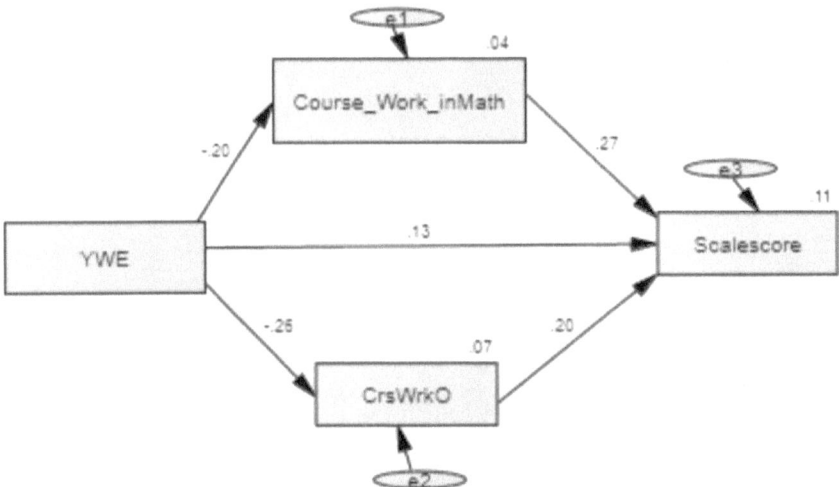

Figure 6.1. The path model focusing on student achievement.
Created by James A. Telese

mediated by Courses taken in Math Methods had a slightly lower path coefficient than Course Work in Math, 0.20 and 0.27, respectively. This indicated that course work in mathematics has a slightly stronger influence on student achievement.

The Path Model Focusing on Pedagogical Content Knowledge

In this model, the following variables were used: Years Teaching, Course Work in Math, Course Work in Math Methods, and pedagogical content knowledge, which is a combination of scores of both LMT Number Concept Raw Score and LMT Geometry Raw Score. The research question posed was "How does teaching experience influence teacher's pedagogical content knowledge mediated by Course Work in both mathematics and others?"

By looking at Figure 6.2, we see the same association pattern as the previous model. GFI is 0.967 indicating the model fits very well. It is not sur-

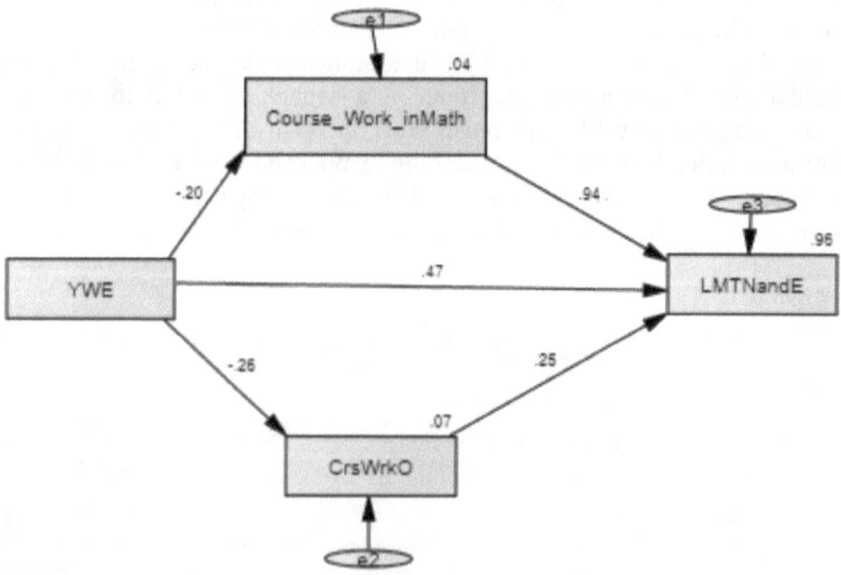

Figure 6.2. The path model focusing on pedagogical content knowledge.
Created by James A. Telese

prising to see that the path coefficient from Coursework in Math has much larger value than course work in math methods on the elementary teachers' pedagogical content knowledge with 0.94 and 0.25 respectively. This model indicated that elementary teachers with more experience had fewer courses in either mathematics or the teaching of mathematics. Teachers' Years of experience has a moderate effect on pedagogical content knowledge.

The Path Model Focusing on Both Pedagogical Content Knowledge and Student Achievement

In this model, the following variables were used: Years Teaching Experience (YWE), Course Work in Math (Course_Work_inMath), Course Work in Math Methods (CrsWrkO), and pedagogical content knowledge (LMTNandE), which is a combination of scores of both Number Concept Raw Score and Geometry Raw Score, and student achievement. The research question that was posed was how does teaching experience influence teacher's pedagogical content knowledge and student achievement mediated by Course Work in both mathematics and others (see figure 6.3).

For this model, the GFI is 0.724, which indicates a good fit. It is very interesting that there are positive associations between Course Work in Math Methods and student achievement, and pedagogical content knowledge and student achievement. However, there is no association between Years Teach-

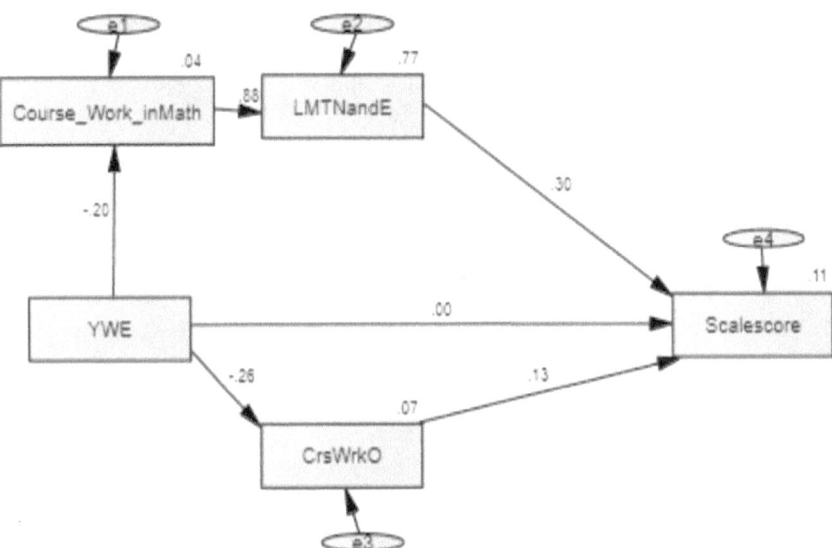

Figure 6.3. The path model focusing on both pedagogical content knowledge and student achievement.
Created by James A. Telese

ing (YWE) and student achievement. This may be due to the strong association of the trajectory from Course work in Math, to Pedagogical Content Knowledge (LMTNandE) to student achievement.

This indicates that mathematics content knowledge together with pedagogical content knowledge has a positive influence nearly three times that of teachers taking only course work in in mathematics education. It would be interesting in a future analysis to use pedagogical content knowledge as a mediator to student achievement.

Comprehensive Path Model

A path analysis was conducted to examine the influence of the professional background variables in relation to student achievement. The model in-

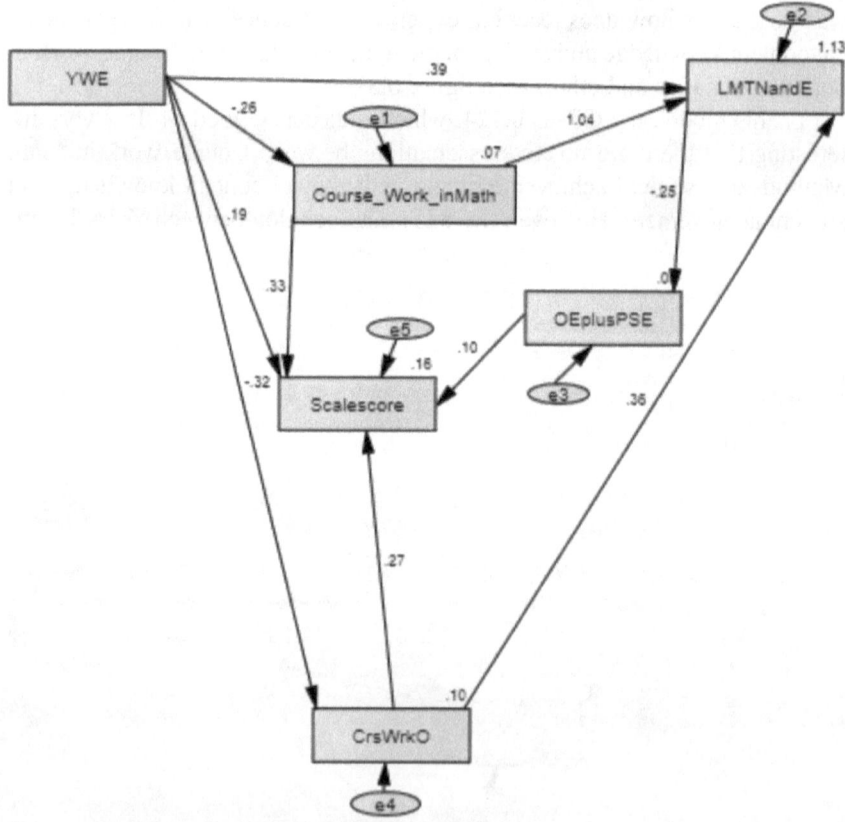

Figure 6.4 The comprehensive path model.
Created by James A. Telese

cluded the following variables: Years Teaching Experience, Course Work in Mathematics, Course Work in Mathematics Education, Pedagogical Content Knowledge, Self-efficacy, and Student Achievement. Figure 6.4 presents a theoretical, comprehensive path model with a GFI of 0.75. The model shows that Course Work in Math (CRSWRKM) when related to Student Achievement (Scalescore) had a path coefficient of 0.33. Course Work in Math Methods had a nearly similar value with a path coefficient of 0.27 when related to Student Achievement.

However, Course Work in Math had a path coefficient of 0.94 to Pedagogical Content Knowledge [PCK] (LMTNandE). Showing an important role content knowledge had on PCK. When Years Teaching (YWE) is mediated through PCK and Self-efficacy (OEplusPSE) and related to Student Achievement, the path coefficient is 0.10. The variable, Years of Teaching (YWE) had a 0.33 path coefficient to Student Achievement.

CONCLUSIONS

The findings appear to be in agreement with those reported in a previous study conducted by Telese (2012). The current study went beyond Telese's study by collecting data at the school level and using direct measures of student achievement and self-efficacy. The path analysis revealed a slightly strong model; yet, the results have important implications for elementary teacher professional development. Student mathematics achievement is influenced by their teachers' years of experience.

Teachers' years of experience play an important role when examining student mathematics achievement. This is a similar finding as that of Harris and Sass (2007). It is assumed often that when teachers have a lot of experience, they become jaded and their students perform less well than others with fewer years of experience. Professional development in mathematics content was strongly associated with pedagogical content knowledge. This finding suggests that it is important for elementary teachers to have an understanding of mathematics in order to have improved pedagogical content knowledge.

As a result, if experienced teachers receive professional development in the form of course work in both mathematics and mathematics education, then there could be a greater chance for improved student achievement. When self-efficacy and pedagogical content knowledge mediate years of experience, the role remains fairly stable suggesting that self-efficacy and pedagogical content knowledge assist in producing higher student achievement in mathematics.

The model indicated that elementary teachers should learn how to teach mathematics since course work in mathematics methods had a moderate influence on student achievement. It appears that if professional development activities are designed to improve pedagogical content knowledge, helping teachers change how they teach elementary mathematics, can develop their self-efficacy and consequently improve their students' achievement.

It is interesting to note the role of experience defined as number of years teaching. Teaching experience was positively related to pedagogical content knowledge, suggesting that as elementary teachers gain experience their pedagogical content knowledge improves. This finding is similar to Harris and Sass (2007) who found that more experienced teachers are more effective in teaching mathematics to elementary students. However, teaching experience was negatively associated with both course work in mathematics and mathematics education. It is unclear what the finding suggests. Perhaps the longer an elementary teacher has taught the fewer courses that are taken. Hence, teaching experience cannot be ignored in student achievement.

Consequently, as teachers' self-efficacy becomes stronger over time, gaining experience, they may strive to change instructional practices based on their experiences as they fully consider the teaching context and the types of students they teach (Grouws & Cebulla, 2000; NCTM, 1991, 2014). A limitation of the study was the small sample size. There is more research that is needed to further delineate the findings with a larger sample of teachers.

ACKNOWLEDGMENTS

The authors would like to thank the principals of the schools who allowed us to conduct the study and the teachers who were willing to participate.

NOTE

1. The authors would like to acknowledge the assistant of the Assistant Superintendent of Curriculum in San Benito Consolidate School District for allowing the study to take place.

REFERENCES

Anthony, G., & Walshaw, M. (2009). *Effective pedagogy in mathematics* (Vol. 19). Belley, France: International Academy of Education.

Ball D., L., Lubienski, S., & Mewborn, D. (2001). Research on teaching mathematics: The unsolved problem of teachers' mathematical knowledge. In V. Richardson (Ed.), *Handbook of research on teaching (4th ed.)*. New York, NY: Macmillan.

Ball, D. L., Thames, M. H., & Phelps, G. (2008). Content knowledge for teaching: What makes it special. *Journal of Teacher Education, 59*(5), 389–407. doi: 10.1177/0022487108324554

Bass, H., & Ball, D. L. (2003). Foreword. In T. Carpenter, M. L. Franke, & L. Levi (Eds.), *Thinking mathematically: Integrating arithmetic & algebra in elementary school* (pp. v–ix). Portsmouth, NH: Heinemann.

Butler, R., & Shibaz, L. (2008). Achievement goals for teaching as predictors of students' perceptions of instructional practices and students' help seeking and cheating. *Learning and Instruction, 18*(5), 453–467.

Copur-Gencturk, Y., Plowman, D., & Bai, H. (2019). Mathematics teachers' learning: Identifying key learning opportunities linked to teachers' knowledge growth. *American Educational Research Journal, 20*(9), 1–39. doi.org/10.3102/0002831218820033

Darling-Hammond, L., & Sykes, G. (Eds.). (1999). *Teaching as the learning profession: Handbook of policy and practice*. San Francisco, CA: Jossey-Bass.

Desimone, L.M. (2009). Improving impact studies of teachers' professional development: Toward better conceptualizations and measures. *Educational Researcher, 38*, 181–199.

Drake, C., Spillane, J. P., & Hufferd-Ackles, K. (2001). Storied identities: Teacher learning and subject matter context. *Journal of Curriculum Studies, 33*(1), 1–23.

Educational Testing Service. (2004). *Where we stand on teacher quality*. Princeton, NJ: Author.

Fetler, M. (2001). Student mathematics achievement test scores, droupout rates, and teacher characteristics. *Teacher Education Quarterly, 28*(1), 151–168.

Franke, M. L., Carpenter, T. P., Levi, L., & Fennema, E. (2001). Capturing teachers' generative change: A follow-up study of professional development in mathematics. *American Educational Research Journal, 38*, 653–689.

Greenwald, R., Hedges, L., & Laine, R. (1996). The effect of school resources on school achievement. *Review of Educational Research, 66*, 361–396.

Grouws, D. A., & Cebulla, K. J. (2000). *Improving student achievement in mathematics*. Brussels, Belgium: International Academy of Education.

Hanushek, E. A. (1996). A more complete picture of school resource policies. *Review of Educational Research, 66*, 397–409.

Harbison, R.W., & Hanushek, E. A. (1992). *Educational performance for the poor: Lessons from rural northeast Brazil*. Oxford, UK: Oxford University Press.

Harris, D. N., & Sass, T. R. (2007). *Teacher training, teacher quality, and student achievement (Working Paper No. 3)*. Washington, DC: National Center for Analysis of Longitudinal Data in Education Research.

Kahle, D. K. (2008). *How elementary school teachers' mathematical self-efficacy and mathematics teaching self-efficacy relate to conceptually and procedurally oriented teaching practices* (Unpublished doctoral dissertation). The Ohio State University.

Kane, T. J., Taylor, E. S., Tyler, J. H., & Wooten, A. L. (2011). Identifying effective classroom practices using student achievement data. *Journal of Human Resources, 46*(3), 587–613.

Kazemi, E., & Franke, M. (2004). Teacher learning in mathematics: Using student work to promote collective inquiry. *Journal of Mathematics Teacher Education, 7*(3), 203–235.

Loucks-Horsley, S., Love, N., Stiles, K. E., Mundry, S., & Hewson, P.W. (2003). *Designing professional development for teachers of science and mathematics*. Thousand Oaks, CA: Corwin Press.

Ma, L. (2010). *Knowing and teaching elementary mathematics: Teachers' understanding of fundamental mathematics in China and the United States* (2nd ed.). New York, NY: Routledge.

Meece, J. L., Anderman, E. M., & Anderman, L. H. (2006). Classroom goal structure, student motivation, academic achievement. *Annual Review of Psychology, 57*, 487–503.

Midgley, C., Maehr, M. L., Hruda, L. Z., Anderman, E., Anderman, L., Freeman, K. E. (2000). *Manual for the patterns of adaptive learning scales*. Ann Arbor, MI: University of Michigan.

Mullens, J. E., Murnane, R. J., & Willett, J. B. (1996). The contribution of training and subject matter knowledge to teaching effectiveness: A multilevel analysis of longitudinal evidence from Belize. *Comparative Education Review, 40*, 139–157.

National Council of Teachers of Mathematics. (1991). *Professional standards for teaching mathematics*. Reston, VA: Author.

———. (2000). *Principles and standards for school mathematics*. Reston, VA: Author.

———. (2014). *Principles to Actions: Ensuring mathematical success for all*. Reston, VA: Author.

Pape, S.J., Bell, C.V., Yetkin, I.E. (2003). Developing mathematical thinking and self-regulated learning: A teaching experiment in a seventh-grade mathematics classroom. *Educational Studies in Mathematics, 53(3),* 179–202.

Penuel, W. R., Fishman, B. J., Yamaguchi, R., & Gallagher L. (2007). What makes professional development effective? Strategies that foster curriculum implementation. *American Educational Research Journal, 44*, 921–958.

Rice, J. K. (2003). *Teacher quality: Understanding the effectiveness of teacher attributes*. Washington, DC: Economic Policy Institute.

Sadler, P. H., Sonnert, G., Coyle, H. P., Cook-Smith, N., & Miller, J. (2013). The influence of teacher's knowledge on student learning in middle school science classrooms. *American Educational Research Journal, 20*(10), 1–30. doi: 10.3102/0002831213477680

Schunk, D. H., & Pajares, F. (2009). Self-efficacy theory. In K. R. Wentzel & A. Wigfield (Eds.), *Handbook of motivation at school* (pp. 35–53). New York, NY: Routledge.

Schunk, D. H., Pintrich, P. R., & Meece, J. L. (2008). *Motivation in education. Theory, research, and applications*. Upper Saddle River, NJ: Pearson/Merrill Prentice Hall.

Shulman, L. S. (1986). Those who understand: Knowledge growth in teaching. *Educational Researcher, 57*, 4–14.

Sowder, J. T. (2007). The mathematical education and development of teachers. In F. K. Lester (Ed.), *Second handbook of research on mathematics teaching and learning* (pp. 157–224). Charlotte, NC: Information Age Publishing.

Suh, J. M., & Seshaiyer, P. (2017). *Modeling mathematical ideas: Developing strategic competence in elementary and middle school*. New York, NY: Rowman & Littlefield.

Tchoshanov, M. (2011). Relationship between teacher knowledge of concepts and connections, teaching practices, and student achievement in middle grades mathematics. *Educational Studies in Mathematics, 76*, 141–164. doi: 10.1007/s10649-010-9269-y

Tchoshanov, M., Lesser, L., & Salazar, J. (2008). Teacher knowledge and student achievement: Revealing patterns. *Journal of Mathematics Education Leadership, 13*, 39–49.

Telese, J. (2012). Middle school mathematics teachers' professional development and student achievement. *The Journal of Educational Research, 105*(2), 102111.

Thompson, C. (2009). Preparation, practice, and performance: An empirical examination of the impact of standards-based instruction on secondary students' math and science achievement. *Research in Education, 81*, 53–62.

Throndsen, I., & Turmo, A. (2013). Primary mathematics teachers' goal orientations and student achievement. *Instructional Science, 41*, 307–322. doi: 10.1007/s11251-012-9229-2

United States Census Bureau. (2019). *Quickfacts*. Retrieved from https://www.census.gov/quickfacts/sanbenitocitytexas

Wilson, S. M., Floden, R. E., & Ferrini-Mundy, J. (2002). Teacher preparation research: An insider's view from the outside. *Journal of Teacher Education, 53*(3), 190–204.

Chapter Seven

Teachers' Knowledge, Perception, Sense of Self-efficacy and Role in Mental Health for Middle School Students

Federico R. Guerra, Jr., Ashwini Tiwari, Nancy Peña Razo, and Lionel Javier Cavazos Vela

Thirty-two percent (17.9 million) of the United States population is younger than eighteen years old (Pew Research Center, 2016). One out of every five adolescents in the United States experience having one or several distinctive characteristics of mental health disorders (Costello, Mustillo, Erkanli, Keeler, & Angold, 2003). Research statistics show that one out of ten adolescents could show an inclination for a severe emotional problem, such as Bipolar Disorder or significant mood disorders. One out of eight has shown a tendency to show severe depression (United States Department of Health and Human Services, National Institutes of Health, National Institute of Mental Health, 2015).

Understanding and addressing students' mental and behavioral needs increased in recent years, but statistics show that one-third of mental illnesses in adolescents are undetected (American Academy of Pediatrics Task Force on Mental Health, 2010). Early detection of mental health problems is complex (Heller, 2015). Families and children experiencing mental health problems face many issues in seeking help for diagnosing and treatment (Cannon, 2012). Early detection and treatment challenges may include lack of awareness of mental health issues, mental health diagnoses, or mental health education. Challenges may include limited or no health insurance or personal finances, as well as parent unwillingness to accept the outcome of child's mental illness diagnosis (Dietrich, Snyder, & Villani, 2016).

The mental health issues of adolescents have not only been addressed in research; they have also caught national attention. In December 2012 in Newton, Connecticut, there was a school shooting at Sandy Hook Elementary School that created President's Obama plan to reduce gun violence. On January 16, 2013, President Obama introduced the "Now Is the Time" plan not only to reduce gun violence but also to improve mental health services for adults and students. The program also included providing "Mental Health First Aid" training to "teachers and other adults who interact with youth to detect and respond to mental illness in children and young adults, including how to encourage adolescents and families experiencing these problems to seek treatment" (p. 14).

THE PURPOSE OF THE STUDY

The motivation for this research investigation was to analyze the knowledge of middle school teachers in student mental health needs, to explore teacher perception of their role in supporting students' mental health needs, and the barriers in supporting the mental health needs of adolescents. The study questions were as follows:

1. What are the levels of teachers' perception of current mental health needs in their school?
2. What are the levels of teachers' knowledge, skills, and training experience in mental health?
3. What do teachers perceive is their role in supporting children's mental health?
4. What do teachers perceive are the barriers to supporting mental health needs in their school setting?

THEORETICAL FRAMEWORK

This study draws on from Bandura's (1977) Social Cognitive Theory. Bandura states that individuals achieve better in conditions where they seem competent, and they are more probable to avoid conditions in which they felt incompetent. Individual's self-perceptions about their role in particular activities influence their effort and perseverance. In his work, Bandura (1997) used the term "self-efficacy" and defined it as "one's beliefs in their capabilities to organize and execute the courses of action required to produce given attainments" (p. 3). Bandura maintains that self-efficacy is a much stronger predictor of action in any task. Bandura argues that individuals with a high sense of self-efficacy challenge themselves by setting higher goals. Such people show abilities and consistent efforts to achieve at higher levels and to overcome barriers to achieve higher goals.

A group of researchers (e.g., Guerra, Tiwarni, Cavazos, Das, & Sharma, 2017; Montgomery and Mirenda, 2014; Sharma, Loreman, & Forlin, 2012) argued that educators' knowledge and skills influence classroom practices . These studies suggest that there may be a strong correlation between teacher' self-efficacy beliefs and student achievement. In research done on general education teachers' beliefs and perspective about special education students, researchers (e.g., Sharma et al., 2012; Shirvani & Guerra, 2015) found that teachers who seem confident in their abilities to offer useful accommodations and medications are more likely to engage in effective classroom practices.

In contrast, the teachers who do not have confidence providing meaningful accommodations and medications to special education students have lower success rates. Thus, to meet the instructional needs of the students with special needs, teachers need individual skills and knowledge besides a sense of confidence that their instructional methods will be successful (Guerra, Tiwarni, Cavazos, Das, & Sharma, 2017; Shirvani & Guerra, 2015).

METHODS AND PROCEDURES

This section introduces the reader to the research design, and methods used in the study. As well, a discussion of the instrumentation, study participants and setting, and procedures is presented. Validity and reliability established for the survey instrument concludes the discussion.

Research Design

The study used a survey design. The study design was created on a criterion-based instrument that estimates teachers' knowledge about mental health needs that affect middle-school students. This study combines the approaches of a similar design to prove how teachers' characteristics of education and experience may have a ramification on their knowledge of mental health disorders/issues. Teachers answered targeted questions about their understanding of mental health needs, challenges in working with students affected by mental illness, and concerns and issues in their daily teaching with the aid of a survey instrument used to gather data.

Reinke, Stormont, Herman, Puri & Goel (2011), created the survey tool that was used in this study. For this study, the researchers examined knowledge teachers have regarding mental illnesses. A correlation of their knowledge with their personal or professional characteristics was further examined (e.g., the level of education, the number of years teaching experience, the number of courses taken in their university educational preparation related to mental health, and inservice training on mental health disorders/issues). Besides survey questions, teachers were given four open-ended questions to understand their perspectives about teaching students with mental health needs in their classrooms.

Instrumentation

The survey instrument included items from several categories: (1) demographic information related to teachers taking part in the study and their school; (2) teachers' knowledge, perceptions, attitudes, and beliefs concerning children with mental health needs; (3) teachers' knowledge, perceptions, attitudes, and beliefs about the ability to teach children with mental health disorders/illnesses; and (4) open-ended questions. Mental health disorders/issues were defined as "any psychological, social, emotional, or behavioral problem that interferes with the students' ability to function." The seventy-four-question survey instrument determined teachers' knowledge and perception of mental health disorders/illnesses and research-based interventions/strategies for their similar characteristic signs and symptoms.

Several specific questions were asked about whether the teacher worked with or taught a student in the past year affected by a variety of mental disorders. Examples of these mental illnesses were aggressive behavior, anxiety, defiant behavior, depression, and attention deficit hyperactivity disorder (ADHD). Questions also pertained to what services were provided for students who had mental health issues or needs; another series of questions asked the teacher if he or she received training in behavioral interventions while attending workshops, during their undergraduate and graduate coursework, and at a staff development session. The questions were formatted on the survey instrument to provide as a yes/no answer.

There were also questions that allowed for responses using a 5-point Likert scale ranging from strongly disagree (SD), disagree (D), neutral (N), agree (A), and strongly agree (SA) format. This format allows for differentiation of what information teachers do not know from an inaccurate assumption or misconception. These specific questions were concerned with (1) perceptions the teachers had about whether they should be involved in addressing the mental health issues or needs of students; (2) the teacher's opinions about whether school administration should take part in addressing the mental health concerns or needs of students; (3) their perceptions about the lack of support their school provides for students with mental health issues; and (4) what barriers students with mental health concerns or needs experience in the school.

Study Participants and Setting

Participants in this study included 241 public middle-school teachers from eight middle schools, grades 6 through 8, in South Texas. Teachers had the following levels of education: 202 earned a bachelor's degree, 38 earned a master's degree, and 1 earned a doctoral degree. The years of teaching experience varied. The following data was reported: 1 to 3 years of teaching experience (41 teachers), 4 to 7 years of experience (44 teachers), 8 to 11 years of experience (51 teachers), 12 to 15 years of experience (27 teachers), 16 to 19 years of experience (14 teachers), and 20 or more years of teaching experience (64 teachers). The average student enrollment for each middle school was 844 students at the time of the study. A vast majority of the students in these middle schools are Hispanic (99 percent), classified as economically disadvantaged (89 percent), English Language Learners (39 percent), and classified as receiving special education services (7 percent).

Procedure

The responses for the investigation were compiled from participating middle-school teachers. The superintendent of schools for the school district was presented a letter requesting permission to survey the certified teaching professionals at the eight middle schools in the school district. After acknowledgment had been received from the superintendent, a meeting was held with the middle-school principals to discuss study aim and implications. Upon receipt of permission from the principals, contact was made with teachers to ask for their willingness to take part in the study voluntarily.

The survey was distributed during the teacher's planning or conference period during the day. Consent from the teachers was given to the investigator, and the survey was distributed. Teachers were asked not to identify themselves or their schools on the survey. The campus administration was not in attendance while teachers completed the surveys. The questionnaires were stored in a secure location. Once the data was collected from the middle schools, data was entered into SPSS predictive analytics software.

Reliability and Validity

The questions on the survey were established based on a comprehensive analysis of relevant studies and literature (Aarons, 2004; Chorpita, Becker, & Daleiden, 2007; Elliot & Van Brock, 1991; National Center for Education Evaluation & Regional Assistance, 2003; Reinke et al., 2011; White & Kratochwill, 2005). The ultimate list and format of the survey questions were based on a series of revisions of the evaluation measure that involved specialists in mental health in schools.

Besides experts in the field, the survey was also given to general education teachers and school administrators, school counselors, school psychologists, and special education teachers for their evaluation, revisions of the content of the survey, question design, and language (grammar) used in the development of the questions. A survey was also piloted at a university that included faculty members and graduate students in the academic field of school-based mental health. The study conducted by Reinke et al. (2011) focused on items teachers reported on mental health concerns in their schools; report of knowledge, skills, and training; barriers and gaps in services; and perceived roles of teachers and school psychologists.

RESULTS

Descriptive statistics were computed in the form of a frequency distribution for categorical items and any issues that might negatively influence data analysis were identified by calculating descriptive statistics, which included the mean and the standard deviation for numeric variables. Table 7.1 shows the results of five demographic questions included in the survey. The total number of surveys returned was 241. There were 151 teachers who completed these four open-ended questions:

- What are the top three areas where you feel you need additional knowledge and skills training?
- What are the main three challenges you face in your job regarding mental health?
- What are some of your concerns related to teaching students with mental health issues?
- What are the most concerning mental health issues in your school?

Table 7.1 comprises the demographic data. The teachers who took part in the survey achieved various degrees of education. The majority of teachers surveyed showed a bachelor's degree as their highest level of education (83.8 percent). Teachers with master's degrees accounted for 15.8 percent, and only 0.4 percent of the participants reported attaining a doctoral degree. The majority of the teachers ($n=64$) had twenty years or more of teaching experience (26.5 percent) and 51 teachers had the second highest with 21.2 percent of years of experience (8 to 11). There were 14 teachers (5.8 percent) who had sixteen to nineteen years' experience, and 11.2 percent responded (n=27) to having twelve to fifteen years.

Table 7.1. Overall Percentage for Demographic Questions

Demographic Question	n	Percentage
Highest Level of Education		
Bachelor's Degree	202	83.8
Master's Degree	38	15.8
Doctoral Degree	1	0.4
Number of Years of Teaching Experience		
1 to 3 Years	41	17
4 to 7 Years	44	18.3
8 to 11 Years	51	21.2
12 to 15 Years	27	11.2
16 to 19 Years	14	5.8
20 Years or More	64	26.5
Courses Taken at a Higher Education Institution Concerned with Any Type of Mental Illness		
0	65	27.3
1–2	104	43.7
3–4	32	13.4
5–6	19	8
7–8	4	1.7
9 or more	14	5.9
As a Teacher—You Have Received School Administration Support in Working with Students Diagnosed with Mental Illness		
Yes	128	53.6
No	111	46.4
As a Teacher—You have Attended Training or Workshops Related to Teaching Students with Mental Illness		
Yes	85	35.9
No	152	64.1

There were 44 teachers that showed they had four to seven years experiences making up 18.3 percent. Forty-one teachers (17 percent) reported that they had one to three years of teaching experience. The "*courses are taken*" section shows that 27.3 percent of the respondents had no prior coursework in their teacher preparation college program pertinent to mental health; 43.7 percent of teachers surveyed took at least one to two courses in higher education coursework dealing with mental health; and 13.4 percent took three to four courses. Eight percent of surveyed teachers took five to six courses; 1.7 percent took seven to eight courses; and 5.9 percent took nine or more courses.

Based on the descriptive data analysis, the majority (71 percent) of the teachers graduated and received a teacher certification with two or less academic courses focused on the instruction of student mental health. Fifty-three percent of teachers surveyed received no school administration support, and

46.4 percent of the middle-school teachers received support from their school administration. In professional development, 35.9 percent of the teachers could attend mental health–related training or attend a workshop, and 64.1 percent did not attend training or workshops related to mental health.

Table 7.2 includes the frequencies for questions related to the mental health issues, teacher knowledge, training, and experience in supporting mental health, and the teacher's role in addressing students' mental health needs.

Table 7.2. Teacher Responses to Survey Questions

Survey Items Description and Responses	%
Types of Mental Health Issues	
Question: Students inhibit mental health issues such as:	
Disruptive behavior—acting out	95
Defiant Behavior	94
Hyperactivity	93
Lack of Focus	92
Peer Interaction Issues	88
Teacher Knowledge, Training, and Experience in Supporting Mental Health	
Question: Teacher Education and Training in Using Behavioral Interventions	
No or Minimal Training	56
Moderate	34
Substantial	6
Question: Teacher Experience in Using Behavioral Interventions	
No or Minimal Training	51
Moderate	43
Substantial	7
Teachers' Role in Addressing Students' Mental Health Needs	
Question: Need Knowledge in Screening for Mental Health Issues	
Agreed or Strongly Agreed	31
Neutral	30
Disagreed or Strongly Disagreed	39
Question: Need Knowledge in Referring Children and Families to School-based Service Providers	
Agreed or Strongly Agreed	49
Neutral	25
Disagreed or Strongly Disagreed	25
Question: Do You Implement Classroom Behavioral Interventions:	
Agreed or Strongly Agreed	46
Neutral	34
Disagreed or Strongly Disagreed	20
Question: Need Knowledge in Conducting Behavioral Assessments:	
Agreed or Strongly Agreed	38
Neutral	28
Disagreed or Strongly Disagreed	33

Types of Mental Health Issues

Teachers identified whether they worked with or taught a student in the past year affected by mental health issues. Common mental health concerns included aggressive behavior, anxiety problems, depression, and defiant behavior. The five most cited mental health problems were (a) disruptive behavior/acting out (95 percent); (b) defiant behavior (94 percent); (c) hyperactivity (93 percent); (d) problems with attention (92 percent); and (e) peer problems (88 percent). Many teachers reported working with students who showed a range of internalizing symptoms, externalizing symptoms, and family issues.

Teacher Knowledge, Training, and Experience in Supporting Mental Health

Teachers rated their education and training in using behavioral interventions. Teachers rated their education or training as none or minimal (56 percent), 34 percent as moderate, and 6 percent as substantial. Most participants did not seem confident in their knowledge and training to use interventions. Besides education and training, teachers rated the extent of experience in using behavioral interventions, with 51 percent rating as none or minimal, 43 percent as moderate, and 7 percent as substantial.

Once again, most teachers reported they did not have experience using behavioral interventions in the classroom. If teachers received training in behavioral interventions, they highlighted the particular format in which training occurred. The top three forms included inservice workshops ($n = 111$), independent reading or self-study ($n = 105$), and undergraduate coursework ($n = 63$).

Teachers' Role in Addressing Students' Mental Health Needs

Teachers rated the extent to which teachers should be involved in addressing students' mental health needs. In response to the questions of "screening for mental disorders," 31 percent of teachers demonstrated they agreed or strongly agreed, 30 percent were neutral, and 39 percent disagreed or strongly disagreed. In response to "referring children and families to school-based service providers," 49 percent of teachers indicated they agreed or strongly agreed, 25 percent were neutral, and 25 percent disagreed or strongly disagreed.

In response to "implementing classroom behavioral interventions," 46 percent of teachers indicated they agreed or strongly agreed, 34 percent were neutral, and 20 percent disagreed or strongly disagreed. In response to "conducting behavioral assessments," 38 percent of teachers indicated they agreed or strongly agreed, 28 percent were neutral, and 33 percent disagreed or strongly disagreed.

Themes from Open-Ended Questions

Besides, multiple-choice questions, table 7.3 includes teacher responses to four open-ended questions. The responses were analyzed based on thematic analysis to understand teachers' understanding in working with students with mental health disorders/issues in regular education classrooms. The analysis of the responses showed overarching themes about mental health disorders/issues.

Table 7.3. Themes from Open-Ended Questions

Question Description	%
Areas of Needed Additional Knowledge and/or Skills Training	
Question: Need for Additional Knowledge and/or Skills Training	
Behavior Intervention / Classroom Management	28
Identifying Students with Potential Mental Health Issues	16
Attention Deficit Hyperactivity Disorder (ADHD)	14
Disruptive Behavior	11
Challenges as a Classroom Teacher on Mental Health	
Question: What Challenges Do Teachers Face	
Lack of Knowledge / Not Enough Training	26
Student identification that Shows Signs/Symptoms of Mental Health Issues	25
Students with Disruptive Behavior	15
Students that are Hyperactive or Diagnosed with ADHD	7
Question: Concerns Related to Teaching Students with Mental Health Illness	
Lack of Teacher Training Concerning Mental Health	23
Lack of Ability to Identify the Student Exhibiting Signs/Symptoms of Mental Health Issues	11
Not Knowing about Mental Health	10
Lack of Classroom Management Techniques	9
Concerns Related to Mental Health Disorders / Issues in the School	
Question: Teacher Exposure to Students in their Classrooms	
ADHD	17
Defiant / Disruptive Behavior	15
Anger Issues	8
Anxiety	7

Areas of Needed Additional Knowledge and Skills Training

The majority of the participants cited that they need more knowledge and/or skills training in the following areas: behavior intervention/classroom management (28 percent); identifying students that may have mental health issues (16 percent); ADHD (14 percent); and disruptive behavior (11 percent). Most teachers indicated that they need information to control the classroom environment from students "acting out" and causing major classroom disruptions. Teachers stated, "I have no training, or idea on how to deal with mental illness," "I need help in identifying students with mental disorders I am stressed out!" "What do I do when these kids do not take their meds?"

Challenges as a Classroom Teacher Regarding Mental Health

The teachers indicated twenty-seven different challenges they face in the classroom environment. Teachers reported that a lack of knowledge / not enough training was the highest percentage at (26 percent). Lack of knowledge or training was followed by how to determine which students in their classroom show signs/symptoms of mental health issues (25 percent); engaging with children with disruptive behavior (15 percent); and working with students who were hyperactive or diagnosed with ADHD (7 percent). Teachers expressed, "Kids with mental health problems have lots of behavioral problems and are tough to control"; and "I have no knowledge who they are, what problems they have, and what intervention will help them." One teacher stated, "I have no knowledge of mental illnesses or how to select those suffering from a mental health issue."

Concerns Related to Teaching Students with Mental Illness

Teachers appeared concerned with the lack of training regarding mental health (23 percent), followed by the ability to identify children that demonstrate signs/symptoms of mental health (11 percent). Not knowing about mental health illness (10 percent) and the capacity to have classroom management (9 percent) were also concerns. Teachers indicated they are "not properly trained to deal with these types of students" or "I do not know to help." This type of teacher responses comprised 23 percent of the replies to concerns related to teaching students with mental illness.

Concerns Related to Mental Health Disorders/Issues in Your School

Teachers responded with thirteen different problems/signs/symptoms that they have been exposed to in their schools. Students who were diagnosed or expressed signs or symptoms of ADHD (17 percent) were a major concern as reported by teachers. Defiant/disruptive behavior (15 percent), anger

(8 percent), and anxiety (7 percent), respectively, were also mentioned as concerns that students at their schools exhibited.

DISCUSSION

In this study, we examined middle-school teachers' perception and knowledge of mental health issues. This study also examined skills and training needed to work with students with mental health concerns. This study examined teachers' perception of their roles in supporting students with mental disorders in their classrooms. Besides a survey, the study used open-ended questions to understand teachers' perspectives on issues related to mental health needs. The data analysis disclosed significant findings. First, most participants reporting not having training in mental health or they considered the training minimal.

Fifty-six percent of teachers said their education in teacher preparation programs and staff development training regarding mental health issues was none or minimal. Within the same realm of mental health disorders and teacher training programs, other researchers concluded an astonishing majority (93.3 percent) of teacher respondents had no awareness of the term ADHD (David, 2013). Several researchers (e.g., Walker, 2012; Shirvani & Guerra, 2015) also showed teachers who received minimal training in educator preparation programs had negative attitudes toward education of students with special needs.

In another study, 60 percent of teachers showed they did not attend training related to ADHD (Guerra, Tiwarni, Cavazos, Das, & Sharma, 2017). Findings from the current study provide additional evidence that teachers received little training regarding students' mental health issues. This finding is significant given most teachers in this study worked with Latina/o students who have higher mental health problems when compared with other ethnic groups.

From the open-ended responses, four themes emerged: (1) areas of needed additional knowledge and skills training, (2) challenges as a classroom teacher regarding mental health, (3) concerns related to teaching students with mental illness, and (4) concerns related to mental health disorders/issues in your school. Teachers identified the lack of knowledge / not enough training in the overall area of mental health as the highest (26 percent) when asked about the overall challenges they faced regarding mental health in their classrooms (e.g., peer-teacher relationships, classroom management).

Concerns regarding having to *teach* (pedagogy, strategies, teaching to specific behavioral issues students exhibited) students with mental health illnesses were at 23 percent. Behavior intervention / classroom management (28 percent) was also mentioned as an area where teachers felt they needed additional knowledge and skills training. These findings suggest perhaps more education in preservice academic training at institutions of higher education is required.

Course-specific objectives in the knowledge and content delivery of mental health disorders and illness for students who receive special education services and have mental health needs is vital. As the survey responses, particularly the findings from open-ended questions informed, most teachers were not trained to deal with students' mental health concerns.

Teacher preparation programs that prepare teachers for pre-K through fifth grade (elementary level), sixth grade through eighth grade (middle-school level), and ninth through twelfth grade (high school level) perform a crucial function in the education of the "whole child." Several of these key attributes include the behavioral, emotional, and mental contentment of all students. Children's mental health covers a broad range of disorders and illnesses, such as anxiety, ADHD, and autism. Some disorders are more likely to manifest when children are at the elementary school level; whereas other mental health issues, such as bipolar disorder, obsessive-compulsive disorder, depression, suicide, and alcohol and drug use may appear at the junior high and high school level.

Importance must be placed on identifying and attending to individual children with mental health problems. This importance will bring to light a focal point of preventing mental health problems among populations of children who are more prone to have high rates of mental disorders, such as Hispanic children who live at or below low socioeconomic levels (Stagman & Cooper, 2010). One of the significant findings of this study is more than half (51 percent) of the teachers did not receive training in using behavioral interventions when working with students with mental health issues. Most teachers (95 percent) also showed they needed information on mental disorders to control the classroom environment when students "act out" and cause major classroom disruptions.

Also relevant to this study, teachers agreed on receiving adequate support from administrators and education for students with mental health issues. However, their position often changes based on the availability of resources, support from school administrators, and their belief system about mental health. Since a significant relationship exists between emotional health and school achievement, schools must address the mental health needs of children (Jones, 2015). Teachers play a vital role in identifying potential mental health issues students may face because students are in classrooms the majority of the school day (Jones, 2015).

The transitional stages of adolescence, between puberty and adulthood, is a difficult period for most, but especially for those young people who experience or have a tendency of affliction with behavioral, emotional, or a mental health disorder, which can be distressing (Johnson, Eva, Johnson, & Walker, 2011). Frequency rates in the United States project half of the adolescents aged thirteen to seventeen are afflicted with one type of mental health disorder, although 28 percent are afflicted by disorders that develop severe, deterioration of everyday functioning and an increased risk of substance abuse and suicidal behavior (Merikangas, He, Burstein, Swanson, Avenevoli, Benjet, Georgiades & Swendsen, 2010). The outcome of having these disorders hurts different personal attributes, such as home life, school, and peer-to-peer society relationships (Connecticut State Department of Education, 2014).

Mental Health Issues in Texas Schools

Spending for mental health in Texas ranks forty-ninth in the United States compared to other states (Texas Medical Association, 2016). There are estimated 519,368 children and adolescents ages seventeen and younger afflicted with a severe emotional disturbance in Texas (Texas Health and Human Service, 2016). In the State of Texas, it is reported there is a shortage of mental health professionals to support the need to address students' behavioral health (State of Texas Health Services. 2014).

State legislation is engaging in an aggressive position in the education of all staff and faculty members of educational systems across Texas. This effort is to help in the recognition by facilitating in screening, identification, and intervention of mental illness in children and adolescents, and guaranteeing adequate means to support (Dietrich et al., 2016).

Assistance from Schools and the Role of Teachers

Professionals in the mental healthcare field believe schools are in a favorable position to assist in addressing mental health and social demands of children and adolescents through various types of interventions (Shum, 2002). Studies have implied students with learning difficulties and issues of mental health are at an increased probability of encountering academic barriers and failure, and inferior social and peer relation skills while in school. These circumstances and unfavorable consequences affect post-education as well (Langley, Bergman, McCracken, & Piacentini, 2004; Poppen, Sinclair, Hirano, Lindstrom, & Unruh, 2016).

A child or adolescent experiencing a problem with social, emotional, and behavioral challenges has an increased probability of experiencing adverse outcomes to their ability to assimilate into society. (Cannon, Gregory, & Waterstone, 2013). Although children and adolescents may have disciplinary issues in and outside of the classroom environments, students may experience admittance into rehabilitation facilities for alcohol and illegal drug use; an increased chance of truancy, suspensions, expulsions, and dropping out of school; and danger of placement, or referral to the juvenile justice system (Dietrich, et al., 2016).

Having teachers to help serve students with mental health issues—recognizing mental health issues as well as problematic issues—are critical to ensuring student success. Adolescent mental health in schools is a focal point of concern, as schools are perceived as an essential environment for implementing mental health advocacy and dispensing help to teenagers encountering issues in mental health (Anglin, 2003). There are significant voids in research analyzing the beliefs and knowledge of teachers concerning mental health issues among students.

The research literature is limited when appraising the schoolteachers' perspective relating to mental disorders in their classrooms. For example, schools are struggling to identify effective interventions and skills that support the needs of students that exhibit problems in the areas of mental and behavioral health (Davis, Jivanjee, & Koroloff, 2010; Poppen et al., 2016). There is also a lack of healthcare professionals hired by school districts, who can provide mental health services. Findings highlight the lack of information and appropriate professional development many teachers receive and their concerns that they are ill prepared to address the mental health needs of their students (Askell-Williams & Cefai, 2015; Whitley & Gooderham, 2016).

In a previous study, Reinke et al. (2011) examined the perceptions and understanding of 292 elementary school teachers to report critical data on how they perceived their function in the administration of mental health assistance. Reinke et al. considered the significance of collaborating with school administration and special education professionals on students' self-efficacy development to enhance the support and the application of useful skills and procedures. Informed educators in mental health can see the improvement in academic achievement and self-confidence when they can help and provide knowledge regarding mental health vital to implementing successful methods and dealing with expected obstacles (Conner, Miles, & Pope, 2014).

The Mental Health First Aid (MHFA) training, which is a program the National Council for Behavioral Health (2014) has spearheaded is an eight-hour public education in-person training program that is evidence-based. It instructs someone to identify and react to the threatening indications of mental and substance use disorders and connect people with appropriate treatment. MHFA increases the understanding that mental illnesses are real, universal, and treatable. The version of the training pertinent to working with youth is known as Youth Mental Health First Aid (YMHFA).

In 2013, the *Mental Health First Aid Act of 2013, H.R. 1877*, was introduced in 113th Congress to fund states for MHFA training. The act did not pass that year, so the 114th Congress also added it, and it is now referred to as the Mental Health First Aid Act of 2016. The bill was referred to the Committee on Health, Education, and Pensions (114th Congress, 2016). Mental Health First Aid USA cited (2017) during the FY2014 budget, the Substance Abuse and Mental Health Services Administration (SAMHSA) awarded federal grants to 119 state and local education agencies for the training of school personnel in MHFA. In the FY2015 budget, the federal grants were awarded to seventy community-based organizations for training in MHFA.

According to the National Council on Behavioral Health (2014), during the 2013–2014 legislation "21 states passed a law or started executive programs related to Mental Health First Aid" (2014). Of these states, eight adopted a law as a goal for educators or school personnel or mentioned training in YMHFA. One of those states was Texas.

In May 2013, the 83rd Legislature of the State of Texas passed House Bill 3793, which shows an "educator" can receive up to twelve hours of their continuing education by "participating in a mental health first aid training program" (p. 1). The training must address the following:

1. the potential risk factors and warning signs of various mental illnesses, including depression, anxiety, trauma, psychosis, eating disorders, substance abuse disorders, moreover, self-injury;
2. the prevalence of different mental illnesses in the United States and the need to reduce the stigma associated with mental illness;
3. an action plan for use by the employees or contractors that involve the use of skills, resources, and knowledge to assess a situation and develop and implement an appropriate intervention to help an individual experiencing a mental health crisis obtain appropriate professional care; and
4. the evidence-based professional, peer, social, and self-help resources are available to help individuals with mental illness. (TAC, p. 10)

Besides training, the bill addresses ways in which local mental health authority (LMHA) can get funding for training, effective September 1, 2013. In August 2014, the Texas Department of State Health Services (DSHS) reported since December 2013; there were 917 educators and 1,588 non-educators who received the MHFA training. In November 2015, the Texas DSHS said 6,527 educators and 4,792 non-educators were trained in MHFA.

In May 2015, the Texas 84th Legislature, Regular Session, amended the term "educator" from the 2013 House Bill 3793 to now include "all school district employees and school resource officers," effective September 1, 2015. This broadened definition of who needs to be trained was an essential change because other school personnel, and not just teachers, may encounter the mental health needs of students and could help to prevent suicide. The 84th Legislature also enacted House Bill 2186, which addresses training on youth suicide prevention.

As mentioned, researchers show mental health issues in adolescents are on the rise and young people often rely on schools to provide services for mental health concerns. Although earlier studies have used teacher knowledge or perception in comparable domains, such as ADHD or special education practices, there are no studies investigating educators' knowledge or understanding of mental or behavioral health in their schools.

Given the research and the recent national attention to adolescents with mental health concerns, we sought to investigate educators' perception and knowledge in this area in South Texas. Teachers often suffer from stress when trying to manage aggressive and disruptive students, which can lead to burnout and abandonment of the profession (Boulton, 1997). Teachers communicate the urgency for more help, guidance, and instruction to handle students' behavioral problems (Dufrene, Lestremau, & Zoder-Martell, 2014; Boulton, 1997).

Limitations

The results should be interpreted within the context of several limitations. One notable limitation is the small sample size. The current study only included middle-school teachers from a single geographical area, one specific school district, and only middle-school aged (ages eleven to fourteen) students. It is also important to note the current sample was relatively homogenous about ethnicity (99 percent Hispanic). Future research should use a more diverse sample, such as age and ethnicity. Second, as researchers, we could not confirm or deny the diagnosis of any mental health disorders/illnesses. Third, we were not aware of any students who at the time of the survey completion by the teacher were being treated or medicated for mental health disorders/illnesses in the sample middle schools. We did not control teachers' previous knowledge of the diagnostic status of mental health disorders/illnesses. Fourth, this study did not differentiate between different levels of mental health disorders/illnesses; thus, our results cannot be generalized to more severe symptoms of mental health disorders/illnesses. Students could have shown a high rate of the tendency of comorbid disorders associated with any other mental health disorder/illness, giving teachers false disorder symptoms. Another limitation is the sample of participants was only recruited from the United States.

Implications for Practice

The outcome of this study has implications for teacher and school administrator preparation programs in institutions of higher education. Given the proper training, teachers and school administrators can promote critical affirmative connections for support and comprehend the student's behavior and the foundation of their condition. These institutions of higher education should foster a cooperative relationship to provide an outstanding opportunity to increase future educational base and aptitude for future school personnel to recognize and work with students with behavioral, emotional, and psychological needs.

Professional development should be designed and delivered with disorder-specific information, such as characteristics, symptoms, organizing, and planning instruction to best aid the success of student achievement, and practical strategies for promoting positive behavior. The intentional professional development will empower schools to encourage and bolster necessary teacher knowledge, and familiarity may encourage educational achievement for students with mental health issues. Unlike the current results, past research has shown teachers show opposition to the administration of mental health programs or teacher training regarding mental health (Owens, Hoagwood, Horwitz, Leaf, Poduska, Kellam, & Ialongo, 2002; Reinke et al., 2011).

The inadequacy of information or personal educational attainment in mental illness is where teachers may increase their awareness of research-based strategies and disorder components. Having this new knowledge foundation may strengthen and reassure their teaching ability and confidence in interceding for students who may need help. In this respect, post-secondary institutions should collaborate with school districts to provide high-quality professional development training to improve teachers' knowledge, diagnosis, and skills to work with students with mental health needs.

CONCLUSIONS

The findings point to the importance of teachers not having the education, readiness, and training in using behavioral interventions (a) during their pre-service preparation; (b) they also lack confidence in their knowledge and ability to use interventions; and (c) they lack experience in using behavioral interventions. Due to the lack of experience, most teachers reported they did not use behavioral interventions in the classroom.

Findings also showed (a) 31 percent of teachers showed they should be involved in addressing students' mental health needs; (b) 49 percent felt they should refer children and families to school-based service providers for mental health assistance; (c) 46 percent of teachers agreed or strongly agreed with a need for implementing classroom behavioral interventions; and (d) in response to being involved in conducting behavioral assessments, 38 percent of teachers showed they agreed or strongly agreed.

Researchers and teacher preparation programs in higher education could aim to design a program of study that guides teacher inservice candidates in recognizing and comprehending the circumstances concerning mental health. Plans for probable research should concentrate on assisting to increase teachers' knowledge regarding mental health by bringing forth the opportunity for understanding children and adolescents with behavioral, emotional, psychological, and social health issues.

REFERENCES

83rd Texas Legislature (2013). *H.B. No. 3793.* Retrieved August 21, 2016, from: http://www.legis.state.tx.us/tlodocs/83R/billtext/pdf/HB03793F.pdf#navpanes=0

84th Texas Legislature (2015). *S.B. No. 133.* Retrieved August 21, 2016, from: http://www.capitol.state.tx.us/tlodocs/84R/billtext/pdf/SB00133F.pdf

113th Congress (2013). *S. No. 153.* Retrieved April 29, 2017, from: https://www.gpo.gov/fdsys/pkg/BILLS-113s153is/pdf/BILLS-113s153is.pdf

114th Congress (2016). *H.R. No. 1877.* Retrieved April 29, 2017, from: https://www.gpo.gov/fdsys/pkg/BILLS-114hr1877rfs/pdf/BILLS-114hr1877rfs.pdf

Aarons, G. (2004). Mental health provider attitudes toward adoption of evidence-based practice: The Evidence-based Practice Attitude Scale (EBPAS). *Mental Health Services Research 6*(2), 61–78.

American Academy of Pediatrics Task Force on Mental Health. (2010). Enhancing pediatric mental health care: Strategies for preparing a community. Retrieved from http://pediatrics.aappublications.org/content/pediatrics/125/Supplement_3/S75.full.pdf

Anglin, T. M. (2003). Mental health in schools. Programs of the federal government. In M. D. Weist, S. W. Evans, & L. Lever (Eds.), *Handbook of school mental health: Advancing practice and research* (pp. 86). New York, NY: Kluwer.

Askell-Williams, H. & Lawson, M. (2015). Relationship between student's mental health and their perspectives of life at school. *Health Education (Special Edition), 115,* 249–268.

Bandura, A. (1977). Self-efficacy: Toward a unifying theory of behavioral change. *Psychological Review, 84*(2), pp. 191–215.

———. (1997) *Self-efficacy: The exercise of control*. New York, NY: W. H. Freeman and Company.

Boulton, M. (1997). Teachers' views on bullying: Definitions, attitudes, and ability to cope. *British Journal of Educational Psychology, 67*, 223–233.

Cannon, Y. (2012). There's no place like home: Realizing the vision of community-based mental health treatment for children. *DePaul Review, 61*(4).

Cannon, Y. Z., Gregory, M. J., & Waterstone, J. A. (2013). Solution hiding in plain sight: Special education and better outcomes for students with social, emotional, and behavioral challenges. *Fordham Urban Law Journal*, Vol. 41, 2013; UNM School of Law Research Paper No. 2014-14; Harvard Public Law Working Paper No. 14-09.

Chorpita, B. F., Becker, K. D., & Daleiden, E. L. (2007). Understanding the common elements of evidence-based practice: Misconceptions and clinical examples. *Journal of the American Academy of Child and Adolescent Psychiatry, 46*, 647–652.

Connecticut State Department of Education. (2014). *Guidelines for identifying and educating students with emotional disturbances, Section 2: Definition and interpretation—Definition of emotional disturbances.* Retrieved from https://portal.ct.gov>media>SDE>Publications>edguide>ed_guidelines

Conner, J. O., Miles, S. B. & Pope, D. C. (2014). How many teachers does it take to support a student? Examining the relationship between teacher support and adverse health outcomes in high performing, pressure-cooker high schools. *The High School Journal, 98*(1), 22–42.

Costello, E. J., Mustillo, S., Erkanli, A., Keeler, G., & Angold, A. (2003). Prevalence and development of psychiatric disorders in childhood and adolescence. *Archives of General Psychiatry, 60*, 837–844. http://dx.doi.org/10.1001/archpsyc.60.8.837

David, N. (2013). ADHD in Indian elementary classrooms: Understanding teacher perspectives. *International Journal of Special Education, 28*(2), 1–13.

Davis, M., Jivanjee, P., & Koroloff, N. (2010). *Paving the way: Meeting transition needs of young people with developmental disabilities and serious mental health conditions.* Portland, OR: Research and Training Center on Family Support and Children's Mental Health.

Dieterich, C. A., Snyder, N. D., & Villani, C. J. (2017). Functional behavioral assessments and behavioral intervention plans: Review of the law and recent cases, 2017. *Brigham Young University Education and Law Journal, 2017*(2), 195.

Dufrene, B., Lestremau, L., & Zoder-Martell, K. (2014). Direct behavioral consultation: Effects on teachers' praise and student disruptive behavior. *Psychology in Schools, 51*(6), 1–15.

Elliot, S., & Von Brock, M. (1991). The behavior intervention rating scale: Development and validation of a pretreatment acceptability and effectiveness measure. *Journal of Psychology, 49*, 43–51.

Guerra, F., Tiwarni, A., Cavazos, L., Das, A., & Sharma, M. (2017). Examining teachers' understanding of ADHD. *Journal of Research in Special Educational Needs, 17*(4), 247–256.

Heller, T. (2015). *Mandatory school-based mental health services and the prevention of school violence,* 24 Health Matrix 279. Retrieved from https://pdfs.semanticscholar.org/3193/53d8f14ae6646d329171670446ba344a1421.pdf

Johnson, C., Eva, A. L., Johnson, L., & Walker, B. (2011). Don't turn away: Empowering teachers to support students' mental health. *The Clearing House, 84*, 9–14.

Jones, E. (2015). *How schools can support students with mental illness*. Master's thesis. Retrieved December 21, 2016, from http://digitalcommons.brockport.edu/cgi/viewcontent.cgi?article=1599&context=ehd_theses

Langley, A., Bergman, R., McCracken, J., & Piacentini, J. (2004). Impairment in childhood anxiety disorders: Preliminary examination of the child anxiety impact scale-parent version. *Journal of Child Adolescent Psychopharmacology, 14*(1), 105–114.

Mental Health First Aid. (2017). *National Council for Behavioral Health*. Retrieved from https://www.thenationalcouncil.org/training-courses/mental-health-first-aid/

Mental Health First Aid USA. (2017). Now Is the Time Project Aware Mental Health First Aid Grants. Retrieved April 27, 2017, from https://www.mentalhealthfirstaid.org/project-aware-now-is-the-time/

Merikangas, K., He, J., Burstein, M., Swanson, S., Avenevoli, S., Ben-jet, C., Georgiades, K., & Swendsen, J. (2010). Lifetime prevalence of mental disorders in U.S. adolescents: Results from the National Comorbidity Survey Replication-Adolescent Supplement (NCS-A). *Journal of the American Academy of Child and Adolescent Psychiatry, 49*(10), 980–989.

Montgomery, M., & Mirenda, P. (2014). Teachers' self-efficacy, sentiments, attitudes, and concerns about the inclusion of students with developmental disabilities. *Exceptionality Education International, 24*(1), 18–32.

National Center for Education Evaluation and Regional Assistance. (2003). *Identifying and implementing educational practices supported by rigorous evidence: A user-friendly guide*. Retrieved December 19, 2016, from http://ies.ed.gov/ncee/pubs/evidence_based/evidence_based.asp

National Council for Behavioral Health. (2014). *2014 Mental Health First Aid State Policy Toolkit*. Retrieved April 29, 2017, from https://www.thenationalcouncil.org/wp-content/uploads/2014/08/Policy-Toolkit-FINAL.pdf

Owens, P. L., Hoagwood, K., Horwitz, S. M., Leaf, P. J., Poduska, J. M., Kellam, S. G., & Ialongo, N. S. (2002). Barriers to children's mental health services. *American Academic of Child and Adolescent Psychiatry, 41*, 731–738.

Pew Research Center. (2016). *Hispanic trends*. Retrieved November 10, 2016, from http://www.pewhispanic.org/topics/hispaniclatino-demographics/

Poppen, M., Sinclair, J., Hirano, K., Lindstrom, L., & Unruh, D. (2016). Perceptions of mental health concerns for secondary students with disabilities during the transition to adulthood. *Education & Treatment of Children, 39*(2), 221–246. doi:10.1353/etc.2016.0008

Reinke, W., Stormont, M., Herman, K., Puri, R., & Goel, N. (2011). Supporting children's mental health in schools: Teacher perceptions of needs, roles, and barriers. *School Psychology Quarterly, 26*, 1–13.

Sharma, U., Loreman, T. & Forlin, C. (2012). Measuring teaching efficacy to implement Inclusive practices. *Journal of Research in Special Education Needs, 12*, 12–21.

Shirvani, H., & Guerra, F. (2015). Do high school students with different styles have different levels of math anxiety? *Journal of European Education, 5*(3). doi: 10.18656/jee,75891

Shum, L. W. (2002). Educationally related mental health services for children with serious emotional disturbance: Addressing barriers to access through the IDEA. *Journal of Health Care Law & Policy 5*(1), 233–258. Retrieved from http://digitalcommons.law.umaryland.edu/jhclp/vol5/iss1/11

Stagman, S., & Cooper, J. (2010). *Children's mental health—What every policymaker should know*. National Center for Children in Poverty. Retrieved December 21, 2016, from http://www.nccp.org/publications/pub_929.html

State of Texas Health Services. (2014). *The mental health workforce shortage in Texas. House Bill 1023, 83rd Legislature*. Retrieved December 21, 2016, from http://www.dshs.texas.gov/mhsa/announcements/HB1023_Final.doc

Texas Department of State Health Services (2014). *Mental Health First Aid Annual Report: As Required by Health and Safety Code Section 1001.205*. Retrieved August 21, 2016, from https://www.dshs.texas.gov/legislative/2014/MHFA-Annual Report-MHSA-081114.pdf

Texas Health and Human Services Commission. (2016). *Texas statewide behavioral health—strategic plan*. Retrieved December 19, 2016, from https://hhs.texas.gov/reports/2016/05/texas-statewide-behavioral-health-strategic-plan

Texas Medical Association. (2016). *Mental Health Funding*. Retrieved December 19, 2016, from https://www.texmed.org/template.aspx?id=6491

United States Department of Health and Human Services, National Institutes of Health, National Institutes of Mental Health. (2015). Depression (NIH Publication No. 15-3561). Bethesda, MD: U.S. Government Printing Office. Retrieved November 28, 2016, from https://www.nimh.nih.gov/health/publications/depression-what-you-need-to-know-12-2015/index.shtml

Walker, T. (2012). *Attitudes and inclusion: An examination of teachers' attitudes towards including students with disabilities* (doctoral dissertation) Loyola University, Chicago. Retrieved December 21, 2016, from http://ecommons.luc.edu/cgi/viewcontent.cgi?article=1400&context=luc_diss

White, J. L., & Kratochwill, T. R. (2005). Practice guidelines in school psychology: Issues and directions for evidence-based interventions in practice and training. *Journal of School Psychology, 43*, 99–115.

Whitley, J., & Gooderham, S. (2016). Exploring mental health literacy among pre-service teachers. *Exceptionality Education International, 26*(2), 62–92.

Chapter Eight

Epilogue

Toward More Efficacious Teacher Preparation

Patrick M. Jenlink

More efficacious teacher preparation requires teacher educators concerned with a commitment to teaching, a commitment that is predicated on a high level of self-efficacy in teacher educators; preparing the next generation of teachers who embody a high level of self-efficacy requires much of teacher educators. Whether teaching the next generation of teachers or the next generation of students entering schools and classrooms, success in teaching is predicated on self-efficacy. The research supports that the teacher preparation process can influence and shape teacher self-efficacy (Beza, 2016; Chesnut, 2017; Chesnut & Cullen, 2014; Clark & Newberry, 2019; Fathi & Rostami, 2018; Pendergast, Garvis, & Keogh, 2011; Settlage, Southerland, Smight, & Ceglie, 2009; Thompson, Bakken & Mau, 2009; Wolf, Foster, & Birkenholz, 2009).

TEACHER SELF-EFFICACY

Albert Bandura (1977, 1997) set forth the theoretical foundation of self-efficacy in his seminal work to evolve social cognitive theory.[1] Bandura defined self-efficacy as one's beliefs in his or her "capabilities to organize and execute the courses of action required to produce given attainments" (p. 3). Tschannen-Moran and Woolfolk Hoy (2001) defined teacher self-efficacy as a teacher's "judgments about his or her capabilities to bring about desired outcomes of student engagement and learning, even among students who may be difficult or unmotivated" (p. 783).

Furthermore, Woolfolk (2008) defined teacher self-efficacy as a "teacher's belief that he or she can reach even difficult students to help them learn"

(p. 361). Teacher self-efficacy is the belief a teacher holds about his or her own ability to influence learning on the part of students.

Teacher self-efficacy, in the educational context, is considered an important and powerful influence on teachers' overall effectiveness with students. Tschannen-Moran and Woolfolk Hoy (2001) suggest that supporting the development of teachers' self-efficacy is essential for producing effective, committed, and enthusiastic teachers. For teacher educators preparing preservice teachers to enter classrooms in schools, it is important to understand that the context and areas of content are important influences on the formation and judgments of teacher self-efficacy. Teachers with a high level of teacher self-efficacy are shown to be more resilient in their teaching and likely to try harder to help all students to reach their potential.

A more efficacious teacher preparation, toward the goal of preparing teachers with high levels of self-efficacy, requires an attentiveness to self-efficacy beliefs[2] as foundational to effecting change in preparation program purpose. Equally important is the attainability of more efficacious teachers entering classrooms in schools and bringing to play a high level of commitment to teaching toward the success of all students. A more efficacious preparation of teachers is concerned with fostering a level of self-efficacy in preservice teachers concerned with how students are motivated to learn, teaching difficult concepts, learning content material, and monitoring student behavior, among other responsibilities (Clark & Newberry, 2019).

TEACHER COMMITMENT

Teacher preparation programs concerned with fostering self-efficacy in preservice teachers are also concerned with fostering and ensuring that teachers have a high level of commitment to the teaching profession. Teacher educators, in reframing teacher preparation to create a more efficacious preparation experience understand that self-efficacy and commitment are interrelated. The commitment that drives teachers to enter and remain in the classroom as a teacher remains a construct of great interest among teacher educators (Chesnut & Cullen, 2014).

Commitment is a complex, multifaceted construct. An individual's decision to enter and/or remain in the teaching profession stems from beliefs about future self that are developed during the preservice preparation experience (Chesnut, 2017). Teacher educators have a responsibility to ensure that each new generation of teachers develops a set of personal beliefs about what can be successfully and competently performed, the belief in its utility, and emotional awareness and resiliency, as well as a deep sense of self-efficacy (Chesnut, 2017, p. 171).

Commitment is required, just as is self-efficacy, to initiate and maintain the courses of action needed to prepare for the professional life of teacher. Commitment in concert with "the malleability of confidence makes self-efficacy an optimal target for intervention in teacher" preparation programs (Chesnut, 2017, p. 171).

Self-efficacy beliefs in relation to teacher preparation, as Bandura (1997) originally posited, are explicitly self-referent in nature for the teacher educator concerned with preparing teachers, these self-efficacy beliefs are directed toward perceived abilities given specific responsibilities; for teacher educators and practitioners, responsibilities aligned with student learning and success.[3] Herein lies the importance for teacher educators to embrace a social cognitive theory perspective of teacher preparation, accentuating the value of human agency in preparing future teachers. As Tschannen-Moran, Woolfolk Hoy, and Hoy (1998) emphasize, cognitive processing is of great importance in the formation of efficacy expectations.

TEACHER AGENCY AND SELF-EFFICACY

Equally important for teacher educators is understanding that human agency[4] is mediated by self-efficacy beliefs, which influence one's choices in teaching as well one's effort and persistence when facing disquieting challenges in the classroom, compounded by one's emotions. Instilling a level of understanding about human agency and mediating influences of self-efficacy beliefs warrants experiences in teacher preparation that expose preservice teachers to their own self-efficacy beliefs as well as providing supportive learning environments wherein preservice teachers are allowed to engage in a high level of self-examination concerning their own human agency as it intersects with self-efficacy beliefs.

One's beliefs as a teacher about the capacity to positively impact his or her situation influence how much effort one puts forth, how long they will persist in the face of obstacles, one's resilience in dealing with failures, and how much stress or depression one experiences in coping with demanding situations (Roof, 2015). Teacher preparation programs, and therein teacher educators, need to focus on the social psychology of situations that preservice teachers will experience upon entering the classroom; preservice teachers need to fully understand the demanding situations and the contingencies of teaching in the real world of the classroom and school.

In this sense, teacher self-efficacy and agency are impacted by emotional stability, or the lack thereof. Roof (2015) explains, "[C]ontingencies are external factors influencing teacher effectiveness. Examples of changing factors impacting teachers are: student demographics, parent engagement, teacher support systems, and the public perception of the teaching profession" (p. 104). Teacher education today exists in a rapidly changing society driven by ideological enactments through policy that often negatively affect the emotive dimension of teaching and undermines human agency. Teacher educators and preservice teachers both can benefit by learning from each other how roles have evolved, especially through the lens of self-efficacy and human agency.

The professional climate of the school and classroom is impacted daily by the changes in society, as well as specific changes in policy and law, such as merit pay based on state mandated testing, a law that limits collective bargaining rights, new policies for evaluation and teacher tenure, mandates on teachers in non-union states that limit salary and benefits, and standardization that limits teacher creativity and pedagogy. Teacher educators have a responsibility to engage preservice teachers in developing a high level of self-efficacy and agency as well as commitment to teaching, which requires understanding the external factors that profoundly affect teachers entering schools and classrooms.

The complexity of human agency and its intersection with self-efficacy is further compounded by the emotional stability of the "teacher self." Emotions often play an interconnected and deciding role in the teaching experience, both for the teacher educator and the preservice teacher.[5] The very nature of promoting self-examination on the part of the preservice teacher is compounded by the teacher educator's own experiences in teacher preparation; challenging long-standing norms in preparation programs as a form of behavioral change brings into play challenges of the existing normative standards and functions of contemporary teacher preparation (Chesnut & Cullen, 2014). Experimenting with course design and methods of instruction can allow participants to openly examine their self-efficacy beliefs.

FINAL REFLECTIONS

Teacher educators must enter the experience of challenging normative conditions in preparation programs with a level of commitment that surpasses the very norms they are responsible for creating, in large part. As well, teacher educators may be present for their preservice teachers and provide the needed support to engage in examining their own self-efficacy beliefs and understanding the importance of self-efficacy beliefs in becoming highly efficacious professionals. As teacher educators, there is a need to instill in ourselves the idea that our beliefs about our own capacities as teachers matters, substantively (Tschannen-Moran, Woolfolk Hoy, & Hoy, 1998). That said, there is an equal need to instill in preservice students this same idea that their beliefs about their capacities to enter the classroom and teach matters, significantly.

Teacher educators with high levels of self-efficacy and commitment to preparing efficacious teachers will tend to challenge outdated normative conditions and engage in experiment with pedagogical strategies and instructional methods toward a deeper understanding of knowledge for teaching, and engage in experimenting with the dynamics of the learning experience through inserting new and divergent social cognitive perspectives aligned with instructional materials and learning activities designed to foster deeper and more secure understandings of the "efficacious self."

NOTES

1. Social cognitive theory is premised on the understanding that individuals are

> ... capable of human agency, or intentional pursuit of courses of action, and that such agency operates in a process called triadic reciprocal causation. Reciprocal causation is a multi-directional model suggesting that our agency results in future behavior as a function of three interrelated forces: environmental influences, our behavior, and internal personal factors such as cognitive, affective, and biological processes. (Henson, 2001, p. 3)

2. Self-efficacy beliefs, as related to teaching and teacher preparation may be characterized as the major mediators for one's behavior as teacher (both teacher educator an teacher practitioner), and equally important, effecting behavioral change within students. The dynamic of teaching and learning, when high levels of self-efficacy are present in the teacher, results in behavioral change in the student. Attention to social cognition in the teaching and learning dynamic is quintessential to effecting successful learning in students.

3. Self-efficacy, as Pendergast, Garvis, and Keogh (2011) explain, influences thought patterns and emotions that enable actions between the teacher and student, within the classroom. As Bandura explained,

> People regulate their level and distribution of effort in accordance with the effects they expect their actions to have. As a result, their behavior is better predicted from their beliefs than from the actual consequences of their actions. (1986, p. 129)

4. Bandura (1989) in his examination of human agency in relationship to social cognitive theory, noted

> ... the exercise of personal agency is achieved through reflective and regulative thought, the skills at one's command, and other tools of self-influence that affect choice

and support selected courses of action. Self-generated influences operate deterministically on behavior (in) the same way as external sources of influence do.... It is because self-influence operates deterministically on action that some measure of self-directedness and freedom is possible. (Bandura, 1989, 1182)

5. Bandura (1977, 1995) explained that if mastery experiences, vicarious experiences and social persuasion occur in the context of a positive (non-stressful) physiological and emotional state, they generally create a higher sense of perceived efficacy related to teaching. He postulated that self-efficacy evolves from four sources:

- Mastery Experiences, which involve gaining hands-on practice (and experiences of success or failure) with a specific behavior in a given social situation, are arguably the most vital source of teacher efficacy.
- Vicarious Experiences involve observing others and learning from their success or failure. When an individual observes and interprets another's actions as successful, his or her teacher efficacy will rise.
- Social Persuasion is most commonly understood as encouragement (or discouragement) from a significant other. When a trusted source informs an individual that he is experiencing success, teacher efficacy is likely to increase.
- Physiological and Emotional States: If, during an experience, a person experiences stress, anxiety or another negative emotional or physiological state her teacher efficacy is likely to decrease. The assumption is that she will equate those negative states with her own capabilities (for further discussion, see Bandura, 1997; Tschannen-Moran et al., 1998).

REFERENCES

Bandura, A. (1977). Self-efficacy: Toward a unifying theory of behavioral change. *Psychological Bulletin*, 84, 191–215.

———. (1986). *Social foundations of thought and action: A social cognitive theory.* Englewood Cliffs, NJ: Prentice-Hall.

———. (1989). Human agency in social cognitive theory. *American Psychologist*, 44(9), 1175–1184.

———. (1995). Exercise of personal and collective efficacy in changing societies. In A. Bandura (Ed.), *Self-efficacy in changing societies* (pp. 1–45). New York, NY: Cambridge University Press.

———. (1997). *Self-efficacy: The exercise of control.* New York, NY: W. H. Freeman.

Beza, A. (2016). The path to more efficacious teacher preparation: the role of adequate coursework and practicum factors. *International Journal of Science and Research Publications*, 6(8), 125–130.

Chesnut, S. R. (2017). On the measurement of preservice teacher commitment: Examining the relationship between four operational definitions and self-efficacy beliefs. *Teaching and Teacher Education*, 68, 170–180. http://dx.doi.org/10.1016/j.tate.2017.09.003

Chesnut, S. R., & Cullen, T. A. (2014). Effects of self-efficacy, emotional intelligence, and perceptions of the future work environment on preservice teacher commitment. *The Teacher Educator, 49*(2), 116–132. doi: 10.1080/08878730.2014.887168

Clark, S., & Newberry, M. (2019). Are we building preservice teacher self-efficacy? A large-scale study examining teacher education experiences. *Asia-Pacific Journal of Teacher Education, 47*(1), 32–47. doi: 10.1080/1359866X.2018.1497772.

Fathi, J., & Rostami, E. S. (2018). Collective teacher efficacy, teacher self-efficacy, and job satisfaction among Iranian EFL teachers: The mediating role of teaching commitment. *Journal of Teaching Language Skills (JTLS), 37*(2), 33–64. doi: 10.22099/jtls.2019.30729.2572

Henson, R. K. (2001). *Teacher self-efficacy: Substantive implication and measurement dilemmas.* Invited keynote address given at the annual meeting of the Educational Research Exchange, January 26, 2001, Texas A&M University, College Station, Texas.

Pendergast, D., Garvis, S., & Keogh, J. (2011). Pre-service student-teacher self-efficacy beliefs: An insight into the making of teachers. *Australian Journal of Teacher Education, 36*(12), 45–58.

Roof, D. J. (2015). Social foundations of education and teacher efficacy. *The Online Journal of New Horizons in Education, 5*(1), 103–108.

Settlage, J., Southerland, S. A., Smight, L., & Ceglie, R. (2009). Constructing a doubt-free teaching self: Teacher efficacy, teacher identity, and science instruction within diverse settings. *Journal of Research in Science Teaching, 46*(1), 102–125.

Thompson, J., Bakken, L., & Mau, W. C. (2009). Equity education issues facing multicultural education: A longitudinal study comparing multicultural knowledge and dispositions of field-based and campus-based teacher candidates. *Policy Futures in Education, 7*(4), 416–422.

Tschannen-Moran, M., & Woolfolk Hoy, A. W. (2001). Teacher efficacy: Capturing an elusive construct. *Teaching and Teacher Education, 17*(7), 783–805.

Tschannen-Moran, M., Woolfolk Hoy, A., & Hoy, W. K. (1998). Teacher efficacy: Its meaning and measure. *Review of Educational Research, 68*, 202–248.

Wolf, K., Foster, D. D., & Birkenholz, R. J. (2009). Effect of leadership experience on agricultural education student teacher self-efficacy efficacy in classroom management. *Career and Technical Education Research, 34*(2), 119–134.

Woolfolk, A. (2008). *Educational psychology: Active learning edition* (10th Ed.). Boston, MA: Pearson.

About the Contributors

ABOUT THE EDITOR

Patrick M. Jenlink is Regents Professor and has held the positions of E. J. Campbell Endowed Chair in Educational Leadership, doctoral program coordinator, Department Chair, and professor of doctoral studies in the Department of Secondary Education and Educational Leadership, Stephen F. Austin State University. Dr. Jenlink's teaching emphasis in doctoral studies includes courses ethics and philosophy of leadership, research methods and design, and leadership theory and practice. Dr. Jenlink's research interests include politics of identity, democratic education, and self-efficacy theory, and critical theory. He has edited and/or authored twelve books and authored over seventy book chapters. He has also authored and published over 175 peer-refereed articles, and over two hundred peer-refereed conference papers. His most recent books include *The Next Generation of STEM Teachers: An Interdisciplinary Approach to Meet the Needs of the Future (2019)*, *Teacher Preparation at the Intersection of Race and Poverty in Today's Schools* (2019), and *Multimedia Learning Theory: Preparing for the New Generation of Students (2019)*, and *Dewey Studies Handbook* (2019). Current book projects in progress include *Ethics and the Educational Leader: A Casebook of Ethical Dilemmas* (work forthcoming).

ABOUT THE CONTRIBUTORS

Leigh Butler is the assistant dean of the Darden College of Education at Old Dominion University and the director of the Teacher Education Services and Advising. Dr. Butler also serves as the chief certification officer for teacher licensure.

Lionel Javier Cavazos Vela is an associate dean for research and graduate programs at University of Texas Rio Grande Valley in the College of Education and P–16 Integration. He is currently a licensed professional counselor.

Sandra Cooper is currently a professor at Baylor University and teaches elementary mathematics methods courses and graduate courses in mathematics education. Dr. Cooper's research is focused on early number development, children's literature in mathematics instruction, and mathematics learning in informal environments. She is currently president-elect for the Texas Council of Teachers of Mathematics, is a past president of the Association of Mathematics Teacher Educators in Texas, and served as affiliates director as part of the executive board for the national organization of Association of Mathematics Teacher Educators (AMTE). Dr. Cooper has served as executive director for the School Science and Mathematics Association (SSMA), on the editorial panel for NCTM's *Mathematics Teaching in the Middle School* journal, and conference program chair for an NCTM Regional, SSMA national, and AMTE national conferences.

Maria E. Diaz is assistant professor in the Department of Teaching and Learning, College of Education and P–16 Integration at the University of Texas Rio Grande Valley. She received an EdD in curriculum and instruction from the University of Texas at Brownsville. She is currently teaching undergraduate and graduate mathematics and science education courses, and conducting research on attitudes and beliefs of preservice teachers toward science, Latina girls in STEM, and preservice and inservice STEM teachers' self-efficacy.

Colleen M. Eddy is an associate professor and assistant chair in the Department of Teacher Education and Administration at the University of North Texas. Her research interests include teacher preparation and teacher quality in mathematics education. She had nine years of experience teaching mathematics in the high school and community college before becoming a teacher of teachers.

Charlene Fleener is a retired associate professor of reading and former chair of the Teaching and Learning Department, Old Dominion University. She has written extensively on the preparation of preservice teachers and how children learn how to read.

Sarah Quebec Fuentes is currently an associate professor in mathematics education at Texas Christian University. Prior to receiving her doctoral degree, she was a middle and high school mathematics teacher for ten years. She teaches mathematics methods courses for undergraduate preservice teachers across all grade levels, graduate mathematics education courses, and an action research course. Her research focuses on classroom discourse, preservice teacher education, teacher knowledge, educative curriculum materials, teacher self-efficacy, collaboration, and developing fraction sense.

Qing Gao is a PhD student at Texas Tech University, a senior science teacher for more than twenty years, and a director of curriculum and international programs at Shenzhen Secondary School, Shenzhen, Guangdong Province, China. Her research interests include student-centered science teaching reform, teacher development, and global collaboration in science teaching and learning. She played a leadership role in developing reformed curriculum programs and international projects at her school.

Federico R. Guerra, Jr. is an associate professor, and chair in the Department of Organization and School Leadership at the University of Texas Rio Grande Valley. His area of study concerns effective educational leadership and his specialization is in the area of mental disorders, particularly attention deficit hyperactivity disorder, emotional, behavioral, and learning disabilities in connection to neurobiology. Dr. Guerra also has nineteen years of public school teaching and administrative experience.

Julie J. Henry is an associate professor and chair of the Department of Elementary Education and Reading at Buffalo State College where she teaches classes in early childhood, childhood, literacy, and research. Dr. Henry's scholarship examines teacher change.

William A. Jasper received his doctorate in mathematics education from Texas A & M University. Since 2000, Dr. Jasper has taught undergraduate and graduate mathematics courses for mathematics teachers at Sam Houston State University (SHSU) and was selected for the SHSU Excellence in Teaching Award in 2006. He has had multiple publications and has been awarded over $1 million in grant funding since 2000. Dr. Jasper served as the president of the Southwest Educational Research Association, on the National Council of Teachers of Mathematics Professional Development Committee, and on the TODOS board of directors. His research interests include professional development of middle school mathematics teachers, spatial visualization, mathematics for English Language Learners, and mathematical reasoning through problem solving.

Winifred Mallam is a professor in the Department of Mathematics and Computer Science at Texas Woman's University in Denton, Texas. Due to the interdisciplinary nature of her department, she balances her teaching between mathematics education and mathematics courses. Her research focuses on the teaching and learning of EC-16 mathematics. She serves as a reviewer for NCTM publications and her reviews have been published in one of the journals. She is a regular volunteer at state and national mathematics education conferences and served as treasurer for the Research Council on Mathematics Learning.

Yolanda A. Parker is currently a professor at Tarrant County College in Texas and teaches elementary mathematics content courses, developmental math, college algebra and statistics. Dr. Parker's research is focused on culturally relevant pedagogy in mathematics and the use of manipulatives with adult learners. She is a past recording secretary for the Association of Mathematics Teacher Educators in Texas.

Shana Pribesh is an associate professor of educational research in the Educational Foundations and Leadership Department at Old Dominion University. She is interested in the structural aspects of educational inequality and has worked on studies of student/teacher racial matching as well as the consequences of residential and school moving on educational performance. Dr. Pribesh has over two decades of educational research experience having worked with the American Institutes for Research, RAND, Center for Research in Educational Policy, the University of Michigan, and the American Library Association.

Nancy Peña Razo is an associate professor in practice at the University of Texas Rio Grande Valley in the College of Education and P–16 Integration in the Department of Human Development and School Services where she has taught since 2012 She is the school psychology graduate program coordinator and internship director. Dr. Razo teaches courses in assessment of intelligence, achievement, and personality, bilingual and multicultural assessment, as well as ethics and law in school psychology, mental health services in schools, school psychology practicum, and school psychology internship. She is currently a licensed specialist in school psychology in Texas.

About the Contributors

Alison Reddy is an assistant principal in Virginia Beach, Virginia. Before becoming an assistant principal, she taught eleven years in the elementary school setting and was an adjunct instructor for Old Dominion University. She is interested in the impact of informal and formal field experiences on new teacher efficacy. Dr. Reddy earned her PhD in education curriculum and instruction as well as her EdS in administration supervision from Old Dominion University.

M. Alejandra Sorto is an associate professor of mathematics and mathematics education at Texas State University in San Marcos, Texas. She is interested in investigating the impact of teacher knowledge, teaching practices, and professional development in linguistically diverse classrooms. She is the vice president for the International Statistics Education Association and a member of the board of directors of TODOS: Mathematics for ALL.

Judy M. Taylor is a professor in the mathematics department in the School of Arts and Sciences and Education at LeTourneau University in Longview, Texas. Her research interests include teacher education, teacher efficacy, and teaching and learning mathematics. She is a member of National Council of Teachers of Mathematics. She teaches mathematics to future teachers.

James A. Telese is a professor of mathematics education at the University of Texas Rio Grande Valley, College of Education and P–16 Integration in the Department of Teaching and Learning. He teaches undergraduate and graduate mathematics education and research courses. He earned a PhD in curriculum and instruction from Texas A&M University, College Station. Dr. Telese served as a member-at-large on the board of the Southwest Education Research Association. He holds the Miguel Nevarez Endowed Chair for Education Research. His research interests include mathematics teacher professional development, STEM teachers' self-efficacy, preservice elementary teachers' mathematics proficiencies related to problem solving, and assessment.

Ashwini Tiwari is an assistant professor in the urban education department at the University of Houston-Downtown. His research is centered around "examining issues of educational inequity with a focus on special education in the comparative international contexts."

Jian Wang is a full professor and Helen DeVitt Jones Chair in Teacher Education at Texas Tech University. His research interests are teacher mentoring, teacher education, mathematics teaching and learning, and influences of curriculum on teacher learning. His publications have appeared in the following journals: *Educational Researcher*, *Review of Education Research*, *Teachers College Record*, *Teaching & Teacher Education*, *Journal of Teacher Education*, and *Elementary School Journal*. He served as a coeditor and guest editor for professional journals. He conducted an international study on teacher development in China sponsored by the Spencer Foundation and led the designed-based research project to transform teacher education course work and field experiences across several institutions at the USPREP National Center sponsored by the Gates Foundation.

Elizabeth K. Ward is an associate professor and director of field experiences in the Department of Undergraduate Education in the School of Education at Texas Wesleyan University in Ft. Worth, Texas. Her research interests include teacher education, teacher efficacy, and effective clinical experiences. She is currently a board member–elect on the Association of Texas Educators board of directors and serves as the treasurer for the Texas Association of Teacher Educators.

Sherri M. Weber is an assistant professor in the Department of Elementary Education and Reading at Buffalo State College where she teaches classes in literacy connected with professional development schools. Her research examines literacy instruction and teacher self-efficacy.

Trena L. Wilkerson is a professor in the Department of Curriculum and Instruction in the School of Education at Baylor University in Waco, Texas. Her research interests include teacher education, teacher efficacy, teaching and learning mathematics, and lesson study. She is currently on the National Council of Teachers of Mathematics board of directors. She is a past president of the Association of Mathematics Teacher Educators of Texas and served as newsletter editor and member of the board for the national organization Association of Mathematics Teacher Educators. She also serves on committees related to mathematics education for School Science Mathematics Association, Association of Teacher Educators, and Association of Mathematics Teacher Educators.

Zhidong Zhang is an associate professor in the College of Education and P–16 Integration at the University of Texas Rio Grande Valley in the Department of Teaching and Learning. He is an applied statistician and research methodologist. Dr. Zhang teaches graduate research methods courses.

www.ingramcontent.com/pod-product-compliance
Lightning Source LLC
Chambersburg PA
CBHW021845220426
43663CB00005B/404